# Emil

## and the

# Detectives

## ERICH KÄSTNER

TRANSLATED FROM THE GERMAN EDITION BY EILEEN HALL

ILLUSTRATED BY WALTER TRIER WITH
AN INTRODUCTION BY WALTER DE LA MARE

Jonathan Cape

A JONATHAN CAPE BOOK 978 0 857 55029 3

Published in Great Britain by Jonathan Cape,
an imprint of Random House Children's Books
A Random House Group Company

First Published in Great Britain in 1931

Reissued in this new translation 1959

This edition published 2011

1 3 5 7 9 10 8 6 4 2

Copyright © Jonathan Cape, 1959

The Random House Group Limited supports the Forest Stewardship
Council (FSC®), the leading international forest certification organization.
Our books carrying the FSC label are printed on FSC®-certified paper.
FSC is the only forest certification scheme endorsed by the leading
environmental organizations, including Greenpeace. Our paper procurement
policy can be found at www.randomhouse.co.uk/environment

MIX
Paper from
responsible sources
FSC® C016897

Set in Bembo 13/15pt by Falcon Oast Graphic Ltd

RANDOM HOUSE CHILDREN'S BOOKS
61–63 Uxbridge Road, London W5 5SA

www.kidsatrandomhouse.co.uk
www.totallyrandombooks.co.uk
www.randomhouse.co.uk

Addresses for companies within The Random House Group Limited can be
found at: www.randomhouse.co.uk/offices.htm

THE RANDOM HOUSE GROUP Limited Reg. No. 954009

A CIP catalogue record for this book is available from the British Library.

Printed and bound in Great Britain by Clays Ltd, St Ives plc

# Contents

Emil in his Sunday suit

*Here is Emil, in his dark blue Sunday suit. He hates wearing it, and only puts it on when he has to. Navy blue spots so easily. When that happens his mother damps a clothes brush and rubs and scrubs for all she is worth, holding Emil against her knee, and says, "I can't afford to buy you another suit, you know." That reminds him how hard she works to provide for them both, and to send him to a good school.*

# Illustrations

# Introduction

To keep Emil from his friend the reader for a single moment is a dull thing to do. But if anybody has a right to do it, it would be someone who has read his story over and over in the German in which it was originally written, and who knows a good deal about the very latest books written for boys (and girls). That I cannot claim. None the less, the fact that a book is almost bound to be less good in any other language than its own, and yet that *Emil* seems so alive and alert and exciting in English, and also that it is as a story so much of a novelty to me, will perhaps excuse my saying a word or two about it and about *him*.

I said, "alive"; and that is as true, I think, of everybody in the book as it is of the book itself. Erich Kästner has edged so completely into Emil's skin that we see and think through Emil's own eyes and mind, and yet at the same time we know a good deal more about him and what happens to him than he does himself. His story, too, is a story of today. There is nothing in it that *might* not happen (in pretty much the same way as it does happen in the book) in London or Manchester or Glasgow tomorrow afternoon. None the less, Emil is just like the youngest of the three brothers who goes out to seek his fortune in the old folk tales – and gets it, in spite of a mistake or two on the journey. In other words, it is a tale of adventure and romance.

The man in the bowler hat might be sitting in any corner of any railway carriage any fine morning in England, and Emil (or Jack as his name would probably be) in the other. And yet, there is a difference! And though Emil is the hero of the piece, he is as much of a small boy at the end of the book as he was at the beginning – without a trace of the prig. I know of no other story, either, except possibly *The Pied Piper*, so populous with children, and with real children; and when they swarm round the man with the bowler hat like hornets in July, well, it is *then* that the honey is the sweetest, though this may not be very good natural history.

The story proves too in its own headlong fashion that whenever, whatever or wherever you may find them, boys all the world over are first and foremost *boys* – e.g. Gustav, the "Professor", Traut, and the Major and "little Tuesday", and the rest – just as Grundeises are Grundeises!

As for Pony Hütchen, there is probably not a town in Europe, or America either, where she is not to be seen flashing along on her brand new nickel-plated bicycle, and with as many sweethearts as there are spokes in its wheels.

At the last page it is to old friends that we say good-bye; Emil and his mother and his grandmother and all; even though, and quite rightly too, they wouldn't let themselves be used "for publicity purposes". That is one "moral". The other is as pleasant – all jam and no powder: "Money should always be sent by money order".

May Herr Erich Kästner flourish (both as an author and as one of his own characters), and if he will write another story about, say, little Tuesday, or little Wednesday for that matter, I feel sure there will soon be scores of Emils in England with their mouths wide open, eager to swallow it down.

# CHAPTER 1

# Emil Prepares for a Journey

"Now then, Emil," Mrs Tischbein said, "just carry in that jug of hot water for me, will you." She picked up one jug and a little blue bowl of liquid camomile shampoo, and hurried out of the kitchen into the front room. Emil took his jug and followed her.

There was a woman sitting there with her head bent over a white wash-basin. Her long fair hair was loose and hung down like three hanks of wool over her face so that Emil could not see who it was. His mother poured the shampoo over the woman's head, and asked, "Is that too hot?"

"No, that's all right," came the reply, and Mrs Tischbein rubbed it in until it made a foamy white mop all over the customer's head.

When he heard the voice, Emil exclaimed, "Why, it's Mrs Wirth!" She was the wife of the baker, and he knew her quite well. "Good morning, Mrs Wirth," he said, and put his jug down below the wash-basin.

"Is that too hot?"

*Emil's father was a master plumber, but he died when Emil was five. So his mother became a hairdresser, trimming, washing, and setting the hair of all the mothers and girls in her neighbourhood. She has to do all the housework as well, of course, and the washing and cooking. She is very fond of Emil and glad she can earn enough money for them both. Sometimes she sings lively songs. Sometimes she's ill. Then Emil does the cooking. He can fry eggs, and steak and onions too.*

"Well, Emil," she replied, and it sounded as though she was speaking through a mouthful of whipped cream. "I hear you're going to Berlin. You lucky boy!"

"He did not really want to go at first," said his mother, still rubbing. "But what is there for him to do here all through the holidays? Besides, he's never been to Berlin, though my sister Martha has asked us often enough. They're comfortably off, you know. Her husband's in the Post Office. I can't go with Emil, worse luck! The holidays are just my busiest times. But he's big enough to travel alone now, and he can look after himself. My mother has promised to meet him at the station. She's going to wait for him by the flower stall."

"Oh he'll like Berlin, I'm sure of that," declared Mrs Wirth from the depths of the wash-basin. "It's just made for children. We went there the year before last for the skittle club outing. My word, but it's a noisy place! Do you know – some of the streets were as light at night as during the day. And the traffic! My, what a lot of cars!"

"Were there many foreign ones?" Emil asked quickly.

"I wouldn't know about that," Mrs Wirth returned with a shrug and a sudden sneeze caused by soap getting up her nose.

"Emil, you'd better go and get ready," said his mother. "I've laid out your good suit in the bedroom, and if you get dressed now we can have dinner as soon as I've finished Mrs Wirth's hair."

"What shirt shall I wear?" he asked.

"You'll find everything there on the bed. Have a good wash first, and see you put your socks on right way out. You'll find a new pair of laces too, for your shoes. Run along now."

"Oh, all right," he said and took himself off.

When Mrs Wirth had looked in the mirror and satisfied herself that her hair had set perfectly, she went away too, and Mrs Tischbein went into the bedroom, where she found Emil looking very dejected.

"I wonder who invented Sunday suits," he muttered.

"Why?" she asked him.

"If I knew where he lived, I'd just about go out and shoot him, that's all."

"Dear, dear! What a hard life you have! And some children are just as miserable because they haven't got a Sunday suit. Oh well, we all have our troubles. Oh, and before I forget, ask Aunt Martha to lend you a clothes-hanger this

4

evening, and see you hang your suit up on it when you take it off – and give it a good brush first. You can put your old jersey on again tomorrow. It makes you look like a pirate, but that can't be helped. Now, what else is there to see to? Your suitcase is ready packed, and I've wrapped up the flowers for Auntie. I'll give you the money for Grandma when we've had dinner. Come on now, young man, let's go and eat," and she put her hand on his shoulder and pushed him in front of her towards the kitchen.

There was macaroni cheese with ham in it – Emil's favourite dish – and he tucked into it with gusto. Once or twice he glanced at his mother to see if she minded seeing him eat with such relish when he was just going away – but her thoughts were elsewhere.

"Send me a card as soon as you get there," she told him after a while. "I've put one ready, right at the top of the case."

"All right," Emil promised, removing a piece of macaroni from the knee of his trousers as unobtrusively as possible. Fortunately his mother didn't notice, but went on with her last-minute instructions.

"Give my love to them all," she told him. "And look after yourself. You'll find everything in Berlin very different from what you're accustomed to here in Neustadt. Uncle Robert said he'd take you to a museum on Sunday. Mind you behave nicely. I don't want anyone saying you've no manners."

"All right. I promise," said Emil.

After dinner they went together into the front room, where Mrs Tischbein took a tin box out of a cupboard and counted the money in it. She shook her head and counted again.

"Now who did I have yesterday afternoon?" she wondered. "Do you remember, Emil?"

"Miss Thomas?" he suggested, "and Mrs Homburg."

"Yes, that's what I thought. But in that case, the money's short." She took out a cash book in which she kept her accounts and added up some figures. "Yes, eight shillings short," she said at last.

"The gasman called this morning," Emil reminded her.

"Ah, of course! That's it, and now I've eight shillings less than I'd reckoned on, worse luck." She gave a little whistle, as though to blow her troubles away, and took three notes out of the box.

"Look, Emil," she said, "here are seven pounds

– one five-pound note and two one-pounds. Give six pounds to Grandma, and tell her not to be cross because I haven't sent any money lately. Tell her I've been very short myself, but to make up for that, you've brought the money yourself, and I've made it a little more than usual, and give her a nice kiss from me. Can you remember all that? The other pound is for you. You'll need about ten shillings for your return fare, I think, so you must keep that. Offer to pay your share if you have any meals out, and keep a few shillings in your pocket in case anything turns up. Look, I'll put the notes in the envelope of Aunt Martha's letter. For goodness' sake don't lose it! Where had you better put it, I wonder?"

She placed the money in the used envelope, folded it down the middle and gave it to him.

Emil considered the matter and then tucked the little packet away in the bottom of the inner pocket on the right-hand side of his jacket. Then he patted the outside to make sure he could feel it.

"I don't see how it could get out of there!" he said comfortably.

"Well, don't go telling people in the train

that you have such a lot of money on you."

"As if I would!" Emil protested indignantly.

Before putting the tin box back in the cupboard, Mrs Tischbein put some money from it into her own purse. Then she glanced rapidly through her sister's letter again to make sure of the times of the train by which Emil was to travel.

You may possibly be thinking that this is a lot of fuss to make about seven pounds. Well, perhaps it is, and people who earn a hundred or a thousand pounds a month certainly would not think twice about spending that amount. But, believe me, most people earn a great deal less than that, and to anyone who earns, say, thirty-five shillings a week, seven pounds seems a great deal of money to have saved. Plenty of people would think themselves millionaires if they had five pounds to spend, and in their wildest dreams could not imagine anyone actually possessing a million pounds.

Emil's father was dead, so Mrs Tischbein had to work to keep herself and him. She had turned one of her rooms into a hairdresser's shop where she spent her days trimming, washing, and setting blonde heads and brunettes. She had not only to earn enough to pay the rent, the gas and coal bills, and to buy food and clothes for them both, but there were Emil's school fees as well, and the cost of his books. There were also times when she was not well, and had to have a doctor, and like as not he ordered her a bottle of medicine – and that had to be paid for too. Emil used to look after her at such times, and even did the cooking. He sometimes scrubbed the floor too while she was asleep, so that she should not try to get up before she ought for fear the house was going "to rack and ruin".

Well, now that you know all this, you shouldn't laugh at Emil for being rather a good boy to his mother. He was very fond of her, and knew that she worked hard to get the things for him that all the other boys had. He would have felt pretty mean if he had not worked hard at his lessons, or if he cribbed from anyone else in class or played truant. That would have been letting her down, and he would have hated to do that. He hated to do anything that might distress her.

At the same time, Emil was not a prig. He was not even one of those unnaturally good children who seem to have been born old. He had to try really hard to be good, as hard as some people try to give up sweets, or going to the pictures. And sometimes he found it very difficult to stick to his guns. But it was wonderfully rewarding at the end of term when he was able to say that he was top of the class again. His mother was always so pleased, and showed it. And he felt it was something in return for all the things she did for him.

But to get back to the story . . .

"Goodness me, it's a quarter past one!" Mrs Tischbein cried. "Time we were off to the station. The train leaves just before two, you know."

"Come on then, Mrs Tischbein," said Emil, "and I'm going to carry the suitcase, make no mistake about that!"

# Chapter 2

# The Police Keep Quiet

When they got outside, Emil's mother said: "If the horse tram comes along we'll take it to the station."

Just at that moment it came round the corner, and Emil put up his hand to stop it.

In case you have never seen a horse tram, let me tell you quickly what it looked like. It really was rather remarkable for though it looked like an ordinary tram and ran on tramlines, it was drawn by an old cab horse. Emil and his friends regarded that horse as a disgrace to the town. They longed for the day when there would be electric trams in Neustadt with overhead and underground cables, and five lights in front and three behind. But the mayor considered that one horse-power was quite enough to take the tram over its short run. So there it was, and the prospect of getting electric trams was not worth thinking about. Of course, the horse tram didn't have a steering wheel or brakes. The driver just held the reins in his left hand and a whip in his right, and shouted, "Gee up there!" when he was ready to start.

Anyone who lived in the main street could stop the tram right outside his own house by just tapping on the glass partition behind the driver's seat. Then, at a "Wo-back", the horse stopped. The tram company didn't mind this in the least, nor did anyone else, for everyone in Neustadt, including the horse, always seemed to have plenty of time to spare. Anyone who was in a hurry went on foot, anyway!

Emil and his mother got out of the tram at the station and while he was hauling the suitcase off the platform, a deep voice behind them said: "Hullo! Where are you off to? Switzerland?" It was the police sergeant, Jeschke.

"Oh no," said Mrs Tischbein, "My son's going to Berlin for a week to stay with relations."

But Emil had a guilty conscience where the sergeant was concerned and felt quite sick at the sound of his voice. He and some of his school friends had stopped on their way back from a gym lesson in the meadow by the river a few days ago, to stick an old felt hat on the statue of the Grand Duke Charles which stood in the market-place – 'Charles with the crooked face' he was called. Then, as Emil was good at drawing, he had been lifted up by the others to chalk a red nose and a black moustache on the duke's face. He was just adding the finishing touches when Sergeant Jeschke turned the corner of the square, and, although they had all raced off at top speed, they were awfully afraid he had recognized them.

However, Jeschke made no reference to that now. He merely wished Emil a pleasant journey, and asked his mother how she was, and hoped business was good.

All the same Emil was worried, and his knees shook as he carried his suitcase into the station. He quite expected to hear the sergeant call after him, "Hands up, Emil Tischbein! You're under arrest."

Nothing of the kind happened, but of course he might be going to wait until Emil came home again.

Mrs Tischbein went to the booking office for his ticket – third class, of course – and got a platform ticket for herself. Then they went over to the right platform – there were four at Neustadt – to wait for the Berlin train, and they had still a few minutes to spare.

"Be careful you don't leave anything behind, son," she said, "and don't sit on the flowers. Ask someone to put the case on the rack for you

13

when you get into the train – but ask politely, you know."

"I can do it myself," said Emil. "I'm not a baby."

"Very well, do it yourself. And mind you don't go past your station. It's the Friedrich Street station you want, remember, and you're due there at 6.17. For goodness' sake, don't go getting out too soon. The station before yours is the Zoological Gardens station. Be sure you don't get out there."

"Don't worry so, old lady!" Emil returned cheekily.

"And don't you go talking to other people as you do to me," she replied. "And don't throw your rubbish on the floor of the carriage either, when you've eaten your sandwiches. And for heaven's sake, don't lose that money."

At her last words, Emil clutched his pocket in sudden panic, then gave a sigh of relief. "Whoo! Safe so far!" he said.

He took his mother's arm then, and they walked up and down the platform together. It was his turn to be serious, and he said, "Don't work too hard while I'm away, Mum. And mind you don't get ill, because there wouldn't be anyone to look after you if you did. I should have to fly home to you – in an aeroplane. I shan't stay away longer than a week at most. Mind you write to me." Then he gave her a big hug, and she kissed him on the nose.

The slow train for Berlin came into the station, puffing and letting off steam. Emil gave his mother another hug, and climbed aboard with his suitcase. She handed him the flowers and his sandwiches, and asked if there was an empty seat there for him. He nodded, and she repeated, "Remember it's the Friedrich Street station you get out at."

He nodded again.

"Look out for Grandma. She'll be waiting by the flower stall."

He nodded again.

"And be good, you young scamp."

Another nod.

"And be nice to your cousin Pony. I don't suppose you'll recognize each other."

He nodded again.

"And write to me."

"You write too," he added, and the conversation might have gone on like that for hours if the railway had not kept to its time-table. As it was, the guard called out: "All aboard, all aboard", the carriage doors were slammed, and the train drew slowly out of the station.

The scene of the crime – a slow train to Berlin

*It was part of the Berlin train from Neustadt, and some curious things happened in it. A railway carriage is a strange place. Complete strangers sit crowded together in it, and within a few hours they may get to know each other as well as if they had been friends for years. That may be pleasant, or it may not. It depends what kind of people they are.*

Mrs Tischbein waved her handkerchief till the train was out of sight, then turned and walked slowly away. As she still had the handkerchief in her hand she dabbed her eyes with it. But she soon felt better, and remembered that Mrs Augustine, the butcher's wife, had an appointment, and would be waiting on the doorstep when she got home.

# CHAPTER 3

# Alone with a Stranger

As the train started, Emil said good afternoon to the people in the carriage, and raised his cap politely.

"Excuse me, but is that seat taken?" he inquired, though he could see that no one was sitting there.

A fat woman had taken off her left shoe because it pinched her toes, and was holding her foot out and twiddling the toes to ease them.

"Boys aren't often as polite as that nowadays," she remarked to the man sitting next to her, who wheezed at every breath. "Things were very different when I was young."

Emil had heard that sort of remark before, and he took no notice of it now. Some people were always lamenting the good old days, as though nothing was as good as it used to be – even the air which, according to them, used to be much cleaner. But you didn't have to believe them. They were not lying exactly, nor telling the truth. Generally they were just

18

discontented, and thought anything was better than what they had got at the moment.

Emil felt his right-hand pocket, and was not satisfied until he heard the envelope crackle, though the other passengers looked honest enough, and not in the least like thieves or murderers. On the other side of the wheezy man there was a woman, crocheting a shawl, and in the window seat next to Emil was a man in a bowler hat, reading a newspaper.

This man suddenly put down his paper, and brought a slab of chocolate out of his pocket. "Well, young man," he said, holding it out to Emil, "would you like some of this?"

"Oh, thank you," Emil answered. Then, remembering his manners, he took off his cap, bowed and said, "Emil Tischbein's my name."

The other passengers smiled, and the man in the bowler hat solemnly raised it and replied, "Glad to make your acquaintance. My name is Grundeis."

The fat woman who had taken off her shoe asked Emil: "Has Mr Kurshals still got the draper's shop at Neustadt?"

"Oh, yes," said Emil. "Do you know him? He's just bought the land it stands on."

The man in the bowler hat

*Nobody knows him. It's good to believe the best of people until you have reason not to, but I advise you to be rather careful in this case. Better to be safe than sorry. Even a person who seems to be all right may turn out all wrong if temptation comes his way.*

"Is that so? Well, tell him that Mrs Jacob from Gross-Grünau was asking after him."

"But I'm on my way to Berlin now," Emil explained.

"That's all right. It will do when you get home," said Mrs Jacob, wiggling her toes again, and she laughed so that the hat slipped down over one eye.

"So you're going to Berlin, are you?" asked Mr Grundeis.

"Yes, my grandmother's coming to meet me, and she'll be waiting by the flower stall on Friedrich Street station," Emil replied, and he quietly patted his jacket again. The packet crackled, so all was well.

"Have you been to Berlin before?" Mr Grundeis asked.

"No," said Emil.

"You're in for some surprises then. Ever seen buildings a hundred storeys high? No, I thought as much. But you will in Berlin. They've had to fasten the roofs to the sky so that they won't blow away ... Then, if you're in a terrible hurry to get anywhere, you can go to the nearest post office and they'll pack you in a box and shoot you through a tube to the post office in the district you want to go to ... Yes, and if you haven't got any money, you can go to the bank and get fifty pounds in exchange for your brains. Of course you can't live long without your brain – only a day or two – and to get it back you'll have to pay the bank sixty pounds. The doctors too – they've got some marvellous cures ..."

"It sounds to me as though you must have left your own brain at the bank last time you were there," remarked the wheezy man. "Stuffing the boy with such nonsense!"

Mrs Jacob stopped wiggling her toes, wondering what would happen next, and the other woman looked up from her crochet. The man in the bowler hat was annoyed all right, and soon a fierce argument was going on, but Emil did not care one way or the other. He took out his sandwiches, though it wasn't very long since he had had his dinner. He was half-way through the third, and there was a sausage in it, when the train drew in to a big station. Emil did not see the name of it, and could not make out what the porter was shouting up and down the platform, but the wheezy man, the woman with the crochet and Mrs Jacob all got out. Mrs Jacob nearly got left behind because she had great difficulty in getting her shoe on again.

"Remember me to Mr Kurshals," she said to Emil as she finally scrambled out, and he nodded.

After that he and the man in the bowler hat were left alone in the carriage, and Emil began to feel rather anxious. There was something queer about that man. One moment he was giving you chocolate, the next he was trying to make a fool of you with a lot of nonsense. Emil would have liked to check his money again, just to pass the time, but he did not care to risk it, alone with Mr Grundeis, so as soon as the train moved off he went into the adjoining toilet, and took the envelope out of his pocket. The money was still there and he counted it. Then he wondered what he could do to make it safer, and had a good idea. He remembered he had a pin in the lapel of his jacket. He took it out and stuck it right through the envelope and the three notes, and pinned them to the pocket through the lining of his jacket.

"There," he thought, "nothing can possibly happen to it now," and he went back to the compartment.

Mr Grundeis had settled himself comfortably in a corner seat and appeared to be asleep, so Emil did not have to talk to him. He was able to

Emil began to feel rather anxious

look out of the window, which he liked. Trees, windmills, meadows, factories, cows, and waving farm workers went whirling by as though they were set on a huge gramophone record, but watching them got wearisome after a while.

Mr Grundeis went on sleeping, and actually snoring. Emil would have liked to get up and walk up and down the carriage, but was afraid that might waken him, and he did not want to do that. He leaned back in his seat opposite the man, and had a good look at him. It was funny that he kept his hat on all the time, Emil thought. He had a long face, with a small black moustache and a lot of wrinkles round his mouth. His ears were thin and stuck out from his head.

Whoo! Emil jumped. He had nearly fallen asleep, and that would never do. He wished someone else would get in, so that he did not have to be alone with Bowler-hat, but no one did, though the train stopped at several stations. It was still only four o'clock, so there was more than two hours to go before they reached Berlin. He tried pinching his legs, as that always helped to keep him awake during history lessons at school. Then he began to wonder what his cousin Pony looked like now, for he could not really remember her face at all. He only knew that when Grandma and Aunt Martha had brought her to Neustadt – oh, a long time ago – Pony had wanted to fight him. Of course he had refused. She was no more than flyweight then, to his welterweight, so it would have been quite unfair, and he had told her so. Why, if he'd given her one of his uppercuts, they'd have had to scrape what was left of her off the wall! But she had kept on and on about it, until her mother got tired of it, and made her stop.

Ough! He was nodding again, and had nearly rolled off the seat. He pinched himself and dug his fingers into his legs until he was sure they must be black and blue, but it didn't seem to do a bit of good. He tried counting the buttons on the seat opposite. Counted one way there were twenty-four, counted the other, he could not make more then twenty-three. He leaned back, wondering why that was – and so fell sound asleep.

# CHAPTER 4

# A Wild Nightmare

It seemed to Emil all of a sudden that the train was going round in a circle, like a toy train on the floor. He looked out of the window, and saw the engine drawing the train round, and getting nearer and nearer to the last carriage. It seemed to be doing it quite deliberately, like a puppy trying to catch its own tail, and within the black circle of the railway lines he could see trees and a wind-mill made of glass, and a building quite two hundred floors high.

Emil tried to take his watch out of his pocket to see the time, but he had to tug and tug at it, and found himself at last bringing out the big clock from the sitting room at home. On its face was written, '150 hours per mile. Danger: do not spit on the floor.' He leaned out of the window again and saw that the engine was catching up on the last carriage, and they were coming closer and closer together. At any minute now, they would crash. He could not bear to sit still and wait for it, so he opened the door, stepped carefully out, and set off along the footboard towards the engine. He thought perhaps the driver had fallen asleep.

He looked quickly into the carriage windows as he went by, but every one seemed to be empty. There was in fact no one in the whole train but himself and a man wearing a bowler hat made of chocolate. Emil saw him break a piece off the brim and eat it. He tapped on the window and pointed towards the engine, but the man only laughed and broke off another piece of chocolate, and patted his stomach to show how good it tasted.

At last Emil reached the coal bunker, and with a mighty heave pulled himself up and struggled over to join the engine driver, who was sitting on the box seat of a horse carriage, holding reins in one hand and a whip in the other – as though horses were pulling the train. And in fact they were. Nine of them were harnessed to the engine. They had silvery roller skates on their hooves and raced along the tracks, singing a popular song.

Emil shook the man, and cried, "Stop, stop, or there'll be an accident." Then he found it was Sergeant Jeschke he was shaking, and

Jeschke's eyes pierced through him, and Jeschke's voice boomed out.

"Who chalked the moustache on the Grand Duke's face?"

"I did," Emil confessed.

"Who helped you?"

"I won't tell you."

"Then we shall go on for ever driving round in a circle!"

With that the sergeant whipped up his horses so that they reared up on their hind legs, then galloped on faster than ever towards the tail coach. And there, on top of it, sat Mrs Jacob, looking frightened to death, and brandishing her shoes at the horses who were snapping at her toes.

"I'll give you a whole pound if you'll stop," Emil cried.

"Don't talk nonsense," Jeschke shouted back, lashing away at the horses like one possessed.

Emil could bear it no longer. He jumped off the train and turned head over heels about twenty times on his way down the slope, but without hurting himself. He lay there a moment, looking up at the train. It had stopped too, and the nine horses were all turning their heads to look at him. Sergeant Jeschke jumped up then, slashed at the horses with his whip, and yelled, "After him, after him!" And the nine horses leapt off the rails and rushed down the slope after Emil, with the carriages bouncing about like rubber balls behind them.

Emil didn't stop to think. He just ran as fast as his legs would carry him across the meadow, past some trees and over a stream towards the tall building. Now and again he glanced over his shoulder, and saw the train still thundering after him. It drove straight at the trees and smashed them to matchwood. Only one, a giant oak, was left standing – and perched on top of it sat fat Mrs Jacob, swaying to and fro as the wind blew the branches, and crying because she could not get her shoes on.

Emil ran on until he reached the building, dashed through the big black entrance door, and went on running until he came out on the other side. He longed for some quiet spot where he could lie down and sleep for he was tired out and trembling all over, but he dared not stop even for a moment. The train was clattering through the building already, close behind him.

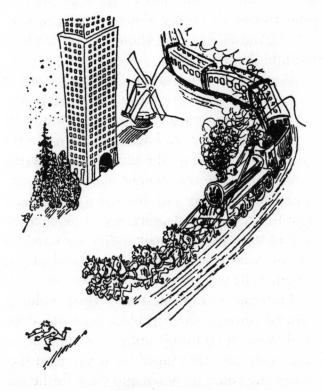

Sergeant Jeschke yelled "After him! After him!"

There was an iron fire-escape ladder going up the outside wall, and Emil started up it without losing a second – luckily he was good at gymnastics. He counted the floors as he passed them, but did not stop to look down until he reached the fiftieth. He turned his head then, and found that the trees had grown quite tiny, and the glass windmill so small that he hardly recognized it. Then, to his horror, he saw that the train was climbing up after him, as though the sides of the ladder were rails. On he rushed as fast as he could go. He passed the hundredth floor, the hundred and twentieth, hundred and fortieth, hundred and sixtieth, hundred and eightieth, hundred and ninetieth, two hundredth – and that was the top. He stepped out on to the roof and stood there, wondering what to do next.

The horses were neighing close behind him. He ran across to the far side. Then, in desperation, he took his handkerchief from his pocket, shook it out and, just as the sweating horses came up over the edge of the roof with the train clattering after them, he spread it out over his head like a parachute, and jumped into space. He heard the train knocking down chimney stacks, then heard and saw no more until, with a crash, he landed in the middle of a meadow.

He lay still for a while with eyes closed, tired out. The quiet of that moment felt like a blissful dream. Yet the feeling of anxiety persisted, and he had to open his eyes to see what was happening up on the roof. He was just in time to see the nine horses opening umbrellas! Sergeant Jeschke had an umbrella too and was waving it about as he urged the horses on. They drew back on their haunches and then took a mighty leap, still pulling the train, and it came floating down towards the meadow, getting bigger and bigger as they came nearer the spot where Emil was lying.

He got to his feet in a hurry, and raced across the meadow to the glass windmill. Through its transparent walls he saw, to his great surprise, his mother washing Mrs Augustine's hair. "Oh, thank goodness," he thought, and ran inside by the back door.

"Oh, Mum," he cried, "whatever shall I do?"

"What's the matter, son?" asked his mother, going calmly on with her work.

"Look!" he gasped, "through that wall!" Mrs Tischbein turned her head just in time to see the horses and the train land in the meadow and come charging towards the mill at a great pace.

"Why, that's Sergeant Jeschke," she exclaimed, greatly surprised.

"Yes, he's been chasing me all over the place," Emil said.

"Why, what have you been up to?" she asked.

"The other day I put a red nose and a black moustache on the face of the Grand Duke Charles's statue."

"Where else would you put a moustache I'd like to know, if not on a face?" asked Mrs Augustine, laughing.

"Nowhere else of course," said Emil. "But he wants to know who was there with me, and I won't say."

"Quite right," said his mother. "Never tell tales – but what are we to do now?"

"Just start the engine, Mrs Tischbein," said Mrs Augustine.

Emil's mother pressed a lever at the side of the table and the four sails of the windmill began to turn. The sun caught the glass they were made of, so that when the horses came up, the blinding light made them rear and shy, and they refused to go another step. Sergeant Jeschke swore so loudly that they could all hear him through the glass walls, but the horses would not budge.

"That will do," said Mrs Augustine. "You can go on washing my hair now. Emil's quite safe."

So Mrs Tischbein got on with her job, and Emil sat down on a glass chair and began to whistle. "This is wonderful," he said chuckling. "If I'd known you were in here, I should never have climbed up that awful skyscraper."

"I hope you haven't torn your suit," said his mother. "And what about the money? Is that still in your pocket?"

These words gave Emil such a shock that he fell off his seat with a crash – and woke up.

# Chapter 5

# The Chase Begins

Emil woke up just as the train was pulling out of a station, and found himself on the floor, feeling very frightened. He must have been asleep, he thought, and slipped off the seat. Now, for some reason, his heart was beating like a sledgehammer. He could not remember where he was at first, then gradually it all came back to him. Of course, he was in a train, going to Berlin, in a compartment with a man in a bowler hat – and he had fallen asleep too.

The man in the bowler hat! That brought Emil's wits back. He sat up and rubbed his eyes. The man was gone. Emil slowly got to his feet, feeling quite shaky. Then, from sheer force of habit, he began to brush the dust off his trousers and jacket – and that reminded him of the money. Was it safe? He could not bear to feel for it in case it was gone. He leaned against the door, too anxious to raise a finger, just staring at the seat where that man called Grundeis had been sitting, and had gone to sleep, and snored. Now Grundeis was gone.

It was silly to take the worst for granted like this, just because the man had left the train while Emil himself was asleep. Naturally the passengers would not all be going as far as the Friedrich Street station where he was to get out. Of course not. And he had pinned the money in its envelope securely on to the lining of his jacket, so surely it must be safe. He had only to put his hand into that inner pocket on the right-hand side ... His hand went slowly towards it ... and felt about in it.

The pocket was empty! The money had gone.

He felt right into the corners of that pocket, and searched frantically through all his other pockets too. He ran his hands over the outside of his jacket – but there was nothing there to crackle. The notes were gone. He gave one last frantic rummage round the inner pocket, and cried out. The pin was still there, and had run into his finger. It stuck in, and left a bead of red blood when he pulled it out.

He wound his handkerchief round the finger, and a tear trickled down the side of his nose – not because of the pinprick, of course. He did not cry for such trifles. Why, a fortnight ago he ran into a lamppost so hard that he almost knocked it over. He still had the bruise on his forehead, and even that hadn't made him cry.

No, it was the money, and because of his mother. You can understand that. It had taken his mother months to save that seven pounds to take him to Berlin. He knew all about that – yet he had fallen asleep as soon as he was in the train! And while he was having that crazy dream, that pig of a man was actually stealing the money. It was enough to make anyone cry. What was to be done about it? Had he got to go on to Berlin and say to his grandmother, "I've come, but I may as well tell you right away that I haven't brought any money, and I'm afraid you'll even have to give me some to buy my return ticket when I go home again."

He could not do that. But the money was gone and Grandma would not get a penny of it. How could he go and stay there after that? But he couldn't go home again either. And all because of a low, mean chap who offered you chocolate, and then pretended to be asleep so that he could steal your money. It really was a terrible thing to have happened.

But Emil soon sniffed back the tears

and looked about him. He might pull the communication cord, and the train would stop and the guard come along to find out what was wrong.

"What's the matter?" he'd ask, and Emil would tell him:

"My money's been stolen."

But as like as not, the guard would only say, "Well, better take care of it next time!" Then he'd be sure to ask for Emil's name and address.

"We shall have to write to your mother," he'd say. "Penalty for improper use of the communication cord – five pounds. She'll have to pay up, you know. Now get back into the train – quick."

Express trains have corridors so that passengers can walk from one end to the other. If Emil had been on one of those, he could have gone along to the guard's van straight away and reported the theft. But his was a slow train. It had no corridor, and there was nothing he could do until it stopped at the next station. By that time the man in the bowler hat might be miles away. Emil had no idea when he had left the train. He began to wonder what the time was, and how soon they would reach Berlin.

Out of the window he could see blocks of

flats and houses with flower gardens, and then a lot of dirty red chimney stacks. Perhaps it was Berlin. He would go and find the guard at the next station, and tell him what had happened – oh, but then of course they would report it to the police.

Oh dear! The police! If he got mixed up with the police now, Sergeant Jeschke would be bound to hear about it and bring up that matter of the statue. "Ah," he'd say, "I have my suspicions about that boy, Emil Tischbein. First he defaces a fine statue here in Neustadt with chalks, then he says he's been robbed of seven pounds on the way to Berlin. How are we to know that he ever had seven pounds? In my experience anyone capable of defacing a monument is quite equal to making up a story like that. He has probably buried the money somewhere, or even swallowed it. Don't waste your time looking for a thief. If there ever was one, it was probably Emil Tischbein himself. I advise you to arrest him at once, Inspector!"

It was horrible. He could not even go to the police for help.

Emil dragged his suitcase down from the rack, and put on his cap. He stuck the pin carefully back in the lapel of his coat, and was ready to get out. He had no idea what to do next, but he could not bear to stay in that compartment any longer. The train slowed down, and through the window he saw rows and rows of shining rails. There were a lot of platforms, too, and he saw porters running along beside the carriages, ready to help people with their luggage. Then the train stopped.

Out on the platform the name of the station was written up in large letters, ZOOLOGICAL GARDENS. Carriage doors flew open and a lot of people got out. Some had friends waiting for them, and they waved and called to one another.

Emil leaned out of the window of his carriage to look for the guard. Then suddenly, a little distance away in the stream of departing passengers, he saw a bowler hat. At once he thought – "*Ah! Mr Grundeis!*" Had he not left the train after all, but only skipped out of one compartment and into another while the train stopped and Emil was asleep? Without another thought, Emil was out on the platform. He forgot the flowers on the luggage rack, but just had time to scramble back after them, dashing in and out of the train as quickly as he could. Then, flowers in one hand and suitcase in the other, he scurried off towards the exit. People leaving the train were packed tight near the barrier, and could hardly move. In the crush, Emil found he had lost sight of the bowler hat, but he blundered on, stumbling round people's legs and bumping into them with his suitcase; but he kept doggedly on till he saw it again. But then, all at once there were two bowler hats.

The suitcase was so heavy it slowed Emil down terribly, but it might get stolen if he put it down somewhere so that he could run after his man. He just had to plunge on, and at last came nearly level with the bowler hats. But which was the right one? One man seemed too short. Emil twisted in and out of the crowd after the other, like a Red Indian on the trail, and was just in time to see his man push through the barrier, evidently in a great hurry.

"Just you wait, you dirty rotten thief," he thought to himself, "I'll catch you yet."

He gave up his ticket, changed the suitcase to his other hand, wedged the flowers firmly under his right arm, and ran down the stairs.

"Now for it!" he thought.

# CHAPTER 6

# Keeping Watch on a Tram

Of course Emil would have liked to rush straight up to the man and shout, "Hand over my money!" But Grundeis did not look the type who would reply civilly, "With pleasure, my dear boy. Here it is. I'm terribly sorry. I'll never do such a thing again." No, it wouldn't be as easy as that.

The great thing was not to lose sight of him now he had found him, so Emil took cover behind a fat woman who was going in the right direction, but kept a sharp look-out from side to side. As he got nearer the bowler hat, he began to wonder what would happen next. When the man reached the main exit he stopped and looked back as though searching for someone in the crowd. Emil kept carefully out of sight, but the fat woman was getting near the exit too. He wondered if she would help him, but knew he could not really expect her to believe his story. Even if she did, the thief had only to say, "Madam, do I look so poor that I'd steal money from a child?" And everyone would start staring at Emil, and saying, "Disgraceful! A boy like that making up such a story about anyone! Children are quite impossible nowadays." The mere thought set Emil's teeth chattering with fright.

At that moment the man turned away and stepped out into the street. Emil set down his bag, and dashed forward to see where he went. His arm ached like anything. That suitcase was a weight! He saw the thief cross the road slowly. Once he glanced back, then went on as though reassured.

A number 177 tram, made up of two cars linked together, drew up opposite the station. The man hesitated, and then got into the front part and sat down in a window seat.

Emil snatched up his case, put down his head, and plunged out into the street. He reached the tram just as it was going to start, but he had time to push his suitcase on to the platform of the rear part, and scrambled up after it – breathless but triumphant!

What next, he wondered? If the thief jumped off while the tram was going, he might as well give up the money as lost for ever. It would be too dangerous to follow him, hampered as he was with the suitcase.

Motor cars rushed past with horns honking and screeching brakes. They signalled right-hand turns and left-hand turns, and swung off down side streets while other cars came swooping up behind them. The noise was indescribable, and on the pavements crowds of people kept hurrying by. Out of every turning vans and lorries, trams and double-decker buses swarmed into the main thoroughfare. There were newspaper stands at every corner, with men shouting the latest headlines. Wherever Emil looked there were gay shop windows filled with flowers and fruit, books, clothes, fine silk underwear, gold watches and clocks. And all the buildings stretched up and up into the sky.

So this was Berlin!

Emil wished he could stop and see every-thing properly, but there was not much chance of that. The man who had his money was sitting there, in the front part of the tram, and might get out at any moment and disappear into the crowds. If that happened, it would be the end of the matter. Emil was sure he could never follow him through all that traffic. Suddenly he got in a panic for fear the bowler hat might have got out already, and he shoved his head out to see. But it was no use, he just had to go on blind, not knowing whether the man had gone or was still sitting in the front car, not even knowing where the tram was taking him. And all this time, he supposed, his grandmother must be waiting for him by the flower stall at the Friedrich Street station! What would she say if she knew that her grandson was travelling round Berlin on a number 177 tram, alone, and in such trouble?

The tram stopped just then for the first time. Emil kept his eye on the car in front, but no one got out though a great many more people got on. They had to push past Emil to get to the seats, and one man complained about his blocking up the gangway.

"Other people want to get home as well as you," he growled.

The conductor, who was taking fares inside, rang the bell and the tram moved off. Emil got pressed back into a corner and someone trod on his foot. Then, all of a sudden, he remembered that he'd no money for the fare, and the conductor was on his way to him. "I'll be turned off if I can't pay," he thought. "Then I shall be done for!" He looked at the other passengers standing all round him and wondered if any of them would lend him the money to pay for his ticket. But they were all deeply engrossed in their own concerns; one reading a newspaper, two others discussing a big bank robbery.

"They dug a tunnel," one of them was saying, "and got inside the bank that way. They cleared everything out of the safe deposits. Thousands of pounds gone they say."

"It would be very difficult to prove what was in some of those safes," observed the other. "Apparently no one's obliged to tell the bank what they deposit in them."

"I suppose," said his friend, "people could claim to have diamonds worth thousands of pounds there when all they had really was a lot of worthless bonds or a few plated spoons!" They both laughed at that.

"That's what will happen to me," thought Emil. "No one will believe that Mr Grundeis stole seven pounds from me. He'll say I'm telling stories and that he only took half a crown. Oh dear, what a mess to be in."

By this time the conductor had got to the platform where Emil was, and called out, "Any more fares?"

The passengers round him handed over their money and in exchange got long white strips of paper punched with holes. When the conductor reached Emil, he said:

"What about yours?"

"Please, I've lost my money," Emil told him, feeling sure the man would never believe it had been stolen.

"Lost it, eh? I've heard that tale before. And how far might you be going?"

"I . . . I . . . I don't know yet," Emil stammered.

"Well you can just get out at the next stop and make up your mind."

"Oh I can't do that!" Emil cried. "I *must* stay on – for a bit. Please let me."

"When I tell you to get off, off you get," said the conductor. "Understand?"

"Oh, give the boy a ticket," said the man who had been reading the paper, and he produced the money.

Emil got his ticket, but the conductor said, "You wouldn't believe how many kids get on every day and pretend they've lost their money. They're only trying it on. I've heard them laugh the moment my back was turned. They think it's a good joke."

"I don't think this one will," said the man.

"Oh no, I won't," Emil assured him, as soon as the conductor had gone inside the tram again. "Thank you very much, sir."

"That's all right," said the man, and returned to his paper.

Then the tram stopped again, and Emil had to lean out to see whether the man in the bowler hat was getting off, but he was not.

"Please will you give me your address?" Emil asked the man with the newspaper when the tram moved on again.

"Why?"

"So that I can pay you back when I have some money again. I'm going to stay in Berlin for a week, so I could bring it round to you. My name is Emil Tischbein, I come from Neustadt."

"Oh, don't bother," said the man. "The fare's paid, and that's all there is to it. Do you want any more money?"

"Oh, no thank you," Emil replied quickly. "I shouldn't like to take any more."

"Just as you like," said the man and went back to his paper.

The tram moved on, stopped, and went on again. Emil discovered that the fine broad street they were in was called Kaiser Avenue, but of course he had no idea where that was. The thief was still in the front compartment, and for all he knew there might be thieves all round him. No one seemed interested, one way or the other. A strange man had paid his fare, but had gone on reading again without even asking why he had no money. Emil felt very small among them all, in that big, busy city. Nobody cared about his having no money, or that he didn't know where he was going. There were four million people in Berlin at that moment, and not one of them cared what was happening to Emil Tischbein. No one has time for other people's troubles in a city. They've all troubles enough of their own. They may listen for a moment, and perhaps say how sorry they are, but they are probably thinking, "Oh, for goodness' sake, don't bother me about it!"

It was awful to feel so alone, and Emil wondered what would happen to him.

# CHAPTER 7

# A Long Wait at the Flower Stall

While Emil was being carried, he knew not where, along Kaiser Avenue on the number 177 tram, his grandmother and his cousin Pony were waiting for him at Friedrich Street station. They stood by the flower stall, as they had said they would, and kept looking at the clock, as more and more people went past them, carrying bags and suitcases, parcels and bunches of flowers – but Emil was not among them.

"I expect he's grown so much, we've let him go by without recognizing him," said Pony, pushing her gleaming new bicycle backwards and forwards as she spoke. She should not really have brought it to the station, but she had begged to so insistently that her grandmother said, "Oh, very well, bring it if you like, you silly girl." So now Pony was all smiles as she imagined Emil's envious eyes when he saw it. "I bet he doesn't know anyone with such a smashing bike," she said comfortably.

But Grandmother was growing anxious.

"What on earth can have happened to the boy?" she said. "The train must be in by now. It's twenty past six."

A few minutes later she sent Pony off to make inquiries, and of course Pony took her bicycle with her.

"Please can you tell me what has happened to the train from Neustadt?" she asked the ticket collector who was standing at the barrier. "It's very late, isn't it?"

"Neustadt? Neustadt?" he pondered, waving his ticket punch. "Oh yes, 6.17. It arrived some time ago."

"Oh dear, are you sure? My grandmother and I have been waiting for ages at the flower stall for my cousin Emil."

"Pleased to hear it, I'm sure," said the ticket collector.

"I don't see what you should be pleased about in that," said Pony, twiddling her bicycle bell so that it tinkled.

The ticket collector made no reply, but turned his back on her.

"Well, you're a queer chap!" said Pony, much offended. "Goodbye."

A few of the people standing about smiled at her, and that annoyed the ticket collector. Pony

Pony Hütchen on her gleaming new bicycle

*The girl on the bicycle is Pony Hütchen – that's a pet name. She lives in Berlin. Her mother and Emil's are sisters.*

wheeled her bicycle back to the flower stall.

"The train came in a long time ago, Grandma," she reported.

"Then what *can* have happened to Emil?" wondered the old lady. "Surely his mother would have sent a telegram if he hadn't been able to come. Do you suppose he can have got out at the wrong station after all? We sent him such careful directions."

"I expect that's exactly what has happened," said Pony, sounding very cocksure. "Boys are so stupid, I bet that's what he's done."

They waited another five minutes on the chance of his turning up, and then as they had nothing else to do, waited for five more.

"I can't see much point in staying here any longer," said Pony at last, "or do you think there's another flower stall somewhere?"

"Well, you might have a look," said her grandmother, "but come right back."

Pony took her bicycle and had a good look round, but she could not see another flower stall. She asked a couple of porters too, and came back quite positive that they had waited at the only one on the station.

"There isn't any other," she announced. "I thought it would be funny if there was. What

54

else was I going to tell you? Oh yes, there isn't another train from Neustadt till 8.33, so we'd better go home now, and I'll come down again on my bike to meet that. If he doesn't show up then, I'll write and tell him what I think of him."

"Oh dear! I don't like it, I don't like it at all," said her grandmother, looking very worried. When she was excited or upset she had a habit of saying things twice over.

"Would you like a ride on the handlebars, Grandma?" asked Pony as they went slowly home.

"Certainly not! Don't be so silly!" said the old lady.

"It's not a bit silly. You can't be any heavier than Arthur Zickler, and he often rides on them."

"If I hear of that happening just once more, I'll tell your father to take the bicycle away for good."

"Oh, you are mean," Pony replied crossly.

When they got home – to 15 Schumann Street – they found Pony's parents waiting anxiously, very worried to hear that Emil had not turned up. Mr Heimbold wanted to telegraph at once to Neustadt, but his wife would not hear of it.

"For goodness' sake!" she cried. "His mother would be worried to death. Let's go back to the station again about eight, and see if he comes by the later train."

"Oh, I hope he will," wailed Grandma, "but I can't help feeling very worried. I don't like it, I don't like it at all!"

"I don't like it either," agreed Pony, shaking her head.

# CHAPTER 8

# The Boy with the Motor-horn

The man in the bowler hat got off the tram at the first stop after it turned out of Kaiser Avenue into Trautenau Street. Emil immediately picked up his suitcase and the bunch of flowers, murmured another "Thank you" to the man who had paid his fare, and got off too. The thief walked in front of the tram, crossed the lines, and proceeded to the other side of the road. When the tram had moved on, Emil saw him standing on the opposite pavement, hesitating, then he went up some steps to a terrace outside a café.

Emil's next move had to be cautious, like a real detective following a suspect. He glanced about him quickly and noticed a newspaper stand at the street corner. It would give him just the right sort of cover, and he hurried over to it. He put down his heavy case, took off his cap and considered what to do next.

The man had taken a seat close to the railing looking down on the street. He was smoking a cigarette, and appeared very pleased with himself. Emil was disgusted to find that a thief could have all the fun, while the person who had been robbed was in such trouble. It made him furious that he – and not the thief – should have to hang about behind a newspaper stand. And it did not make him feel any better when he saw the man ordering himself a drink and lighting another cigarette. But it would be worse still if he got up to go, for there would be nothing for it but to snatch up the suitcase and chase after him again. As long as he sat there, Emil had only to stay where he was – and that he would do even if he had to stay until his beard sprouted! But long before that of course, a policeman would stop and ask him what he was up to.

"Loitering," he'd say. "Suspicious behaviour," and probably, "You'd better come along with me, and come quietly or I'll have to put the bracelets on you."

These miserable reflections were interrupted by a motor-horn which honked loudly just behind him. It made him jump, but when he looked round there was only a boy standing there, laughing.

"All right, don't get the wind up," he said.

"It sounded as though there was a motor right behind me," Emil said.

"Silly chump, that was me. You can't belong round here or you'd know that. I always carry a motor-horn in my trouser pocket. Everyone knows me and my motor-horn."

"I live in Neustadt," Emil explained. "I've only just come from the station."

"Oh, up from the country!" said the boy. "I suppose that's why you're wearing those awful clothes."

"You take that back," said Emil furiously, "or I'll knock you down."

"Keep your hair on," said the boy with the motor-horn good-naturedly. "It's too hot to fight...though if you really want to, I'm willing."

"I don't specially," Emil said. "Let's put it off. I've no time now," and he glanced quickly up at the café to make sure that Mr Grundeis was still there.

"I should have thought you had plenty of time," the boy retorted, "hanging about here with your outside suitcase and that great cauliflower! You looked as though you were playing hide and seek with yourself. I can't say you seem to me in much of a hurry."

"Everyone knows me and my motor-horn."

*His name is Gustav. He is top of his class — in gymnastics! What else?*
*Well, he is good-natured, and always carries an old motor-horn with*
*him. All the children in the district know him, and look on him as*
*their leader. When he runs round the streets honking his horn loudly,*
*the boys leave whatever they are at, and rush after him to see what's up.*
*Usually he is just picking a team to play football, but sometimes the*
*horn comes in useful for other things, as it did in Emil's affairs.*

"As a matter of fact," said Emil, "I'm keeping my eye on a thief."

"What!" exclaimed the boy with the motor-horn. "A thief? What has he stolen? Who from?"

"Me," said Emil, feeling quite important again. "He took seven pounds out of my pocket while I was asleep in the train. I was bringing it to my grandmother here in Berlin. After he'd stolen it, he left our carriage and got into another farther down the train. But I saw him get out at the Zoological Gardens station, and I've been following him ever since. He got on a tram, and now he's sitting over in that café. Look, that's him, looking as pleased as anything with himself . . . that man in the bowler hat."

"Gosh, what a lark!" said the other boy. "Just like the pictures! What are you going to do next?"

"I don't know," Emil admitted, "just keep on following him."

"There's a policeman over there. Why don't you go and tell him about it? He'd look after him for you all right."

"I don't like to do that," Emil confessed. "The police at Neustadt may be after me by now for something I did at home."

"I see."

"And Grandma will still be waiting for me at Friedrich Street station."

The boy with the motor-horn thought hard for a minute, then he said, "Going after a real thief and catching him would be something! Coo! I think I'll help you, if you don't mind."

"I'd be awfully glad," Emil replied warmly.

"That's settled then. By the way, my name's Gustav."

"Mine's Emil."

They shook hands, liking each other tremendously.

"We must get busy," Gustav said. "It's no use just standing about here. We might lose the blighter. Have you any money left?"

"Not a bean."

Gustav gave a little toot on his horn because as a rule that helped him to think, but this time it did not.

"What about getting some of your friends to help too?" suggested Emil.

"Good idea," cried Gustav briskly. "I've only got to go honking round the streets, and the gang will come tearing along to see what's up."

"Go on then," said Emil. "And don't be long in case that chap moves on. I should have to follow him if he did, and you might not be able to pick us up again then."

"Right you are. I'll be as quick as I can," said Gustav. "Trust me. He's eating an egg now, so he can't be leaving just yet. Cheerio, Emil. Gosh, I'm looking forward to this. It's going to be smashing!"

And with that he dashed off.

Emil felt much better after that. Of course it was bad luck about the money – but it could have happened to anyone. Having friends now to help him made all the difference. He kept his eyes resolutely on the thief, who was plainly enjoying the meal – paid for no doubt out of the money Mrs Tischbein had worked so hard to earn. Emil's only fear now was that he would get up and go before Gustav came back.

However, Mr Grundeis obliged him by remaining at the café table, though if he had had the slightest idea of what was being prepared for him, he would probably have ordered a private plane (if that were possible) to get him away.

Ten minutes later Emil heard the horn again and looked over his shoulder. Quite two dozen boys were coming down the street towards him, headed by Gustav.

"Halt!" he cried, as they arrived at the news-

"Well, chaps, this is Emil."

stand. "How's that?" he asked Emil, grinning all over his face.

"Gosh, it's great," said Emil, giving Gustav a delighted dig in the ribs.

"Well, chaps, this is Emil from Neustadt," Gustav then announced, "and that's the rotter who stole his money – over there, sitting by the railings in a black bowler hat. It'd be a nice thing if he was allowed to get away with it, so it's up to us, see?"

"We'll catch him all right, Gustav," said a boy in horn-rimmed spectacles.

"That's the Professor," said Gustav, and introduced Emil to each of them in turn.

"Now let's get a move on," said the Professor. "And the first thing is to see what money we've got."

Each of the boys turned out his pockets and threw all the money he'd got into Emil's cap. One very small boy, whom they called Tuesday, had a whole shilling, and was hopping from one foot to the other with excitement because he was the one to count the money.

"We've got five shillings, and eightpence," he reported. "That's our funds, and we ought to divide it among three of us, in case we get separated."

"Right-o," said the Professor, so he and Emil were given two shillings each, and Gustav took the remaining one and eightpence.

"Thanks awfully," said Emil. "I'll be able to pay you back as soon as we've caught him. What do we do next? I wish I could get rid of my suitcase and these flowers. They're a frightful nuisance when I run."

"Give them to me," said Gustav. "I'll take them over to the café and leave them at the counter. And I'll take a good look at our man at the same time."

"Mind how you go," said the Professor. "If the scoundrel finds out he's being followed, it will make things more difficult for us."

"What do you take me for?" growled Gustav, and went off with Emil's things.

"That chap's face is a sight," he said when he came back. "Your things will be O.K. there, Emil. We can pick them up again when we feel like it."

"I think we ought to have a council of war," said Emil. "But not here, with all these people looking on."

"Let's go to Nicholas Square," said the Professor. "That's quite near. Two of us can stay here to keep an eye on the chap, and we'll have five or six scouts along the road. They can relay any news along to us in no time. If he moves, we'll all come dashing back at top speed."

"Leave all that to me!" said Gustav. "I'll stay here myself and keep watch," he told Emil. "Don't worry. We won't let him get away. You'd better get a move on. It's gone seven already."

Gustav had the boys organized very quickly. The scouts went to their posts along the street, and the rest of the gang, led by Emil and the Professor, ran off to Nicholas Square.

# Chapter 9

# The Detectives Assemble

There was a garden in Nicholas Square, and the boys sat down there, some on two white benches and the rest on the low iron railings set round a patch of grass. They all looked very serious.

The boy they called "the Professor" had been longing for a chance like this. He took off his glasses and polished them with just the air his father wore when he was going to say something very important. His father was a judge.

"It's quite likely," he began, "that we may have to split up on this job, so we ought to arrange for someone to remain at a telephone. Who's on the 'phone at home?"

Twelve hands shot up.

"Who has got the most sensible parents?"

"Me, I should think," said little Tuesday.

"What's your 'phone number?"

"Bavaria 0579."

"Right. Here's a pencil and some paper.

Krumm, you tear up the paper into twenty slips, and write Tuesday's phone number on each of them. And write so that we can all read it, see? Then hand them round. That will be our reporting station. Tuesday must be kept informed there, all the time, of what's going on, where everyone is, and what he's doing. Then anyone who wants information simply rings up Tuesday and gets it."

"But I shan't be at home," Tuesday exclaimed in horror.

"Yes, you will," said the Professor. "As soon as we've finished planning things you'll go right home and stay there with your ear glued to the telephone."

"But I want to be there when the thief's caught," Tuesday protested. "I'm small and I might be very useful."

"No, you go home and attend to the telephone," insisted the Professor. "That's useful and very important."

"Oh, all right, if you say so," Tuesday agreed reluctantly.

Krumm handed round the slips of paper, and each tucked his safely away in a pocket. One or two, who were very thorough, learned the number by heart at once.

"We ought to have – sort of reserves to fall back on," said Emil.

"Of course," agreed the Professor. "Anyone not actually taking part in the chase is to stay here in Nicholas Square. And you'd better take it in turns to go home and say you may be out late. You might even say you were going to spend the night with a friend – that would make it easier if we have to keep going till morning. Emil, Gustav, Krumm, you two Mittlers and I will be the front-line force. We'd better ring up our homes at once and say we'll be late. What else? Oh, yes. Traut, you be messenger. Go home with Tuesday, and be ready to go at once to Nicholas Square if we send for you. Well, now we've got our detectives, reserves, a telephone service and a messenger. Those are the most important things for the moment, I think."

"We shall need something to eat," Emil put in practically. "Perhaps some of your chaps could go home and fetch some food."

"Who lives nearest?" asked the Professor, looking them over. "The Mittlers, Gerold, Frederick the First, Brunner and Meyer – you run home and bring back what you can in the way of food." Those named ran off at once.

"You really are a lot of mugs," Traut exclaimed suddenly. "You keep on talking about food and telephones and spending the night away from home, and haven't said a word about how the thief is to be caught. You are a lot of ... of gas-bags!" He could not think of a worse insult.

"Have you got any stuff for taking his fingerprints?" asked Peters. He had seen so many thrillers at the cinema that it had rather gone to his head. "Of course," he added, "he may have worn rubber gloves, and then no one will be able to prove anything against him."

"Don't be an idiot," said Traut. "We'll just have to keep an eye on him, and wait for a chance to sneak the money back."

"Oh no, that won't do at all!" exclaimed the Professor. "If we take the money from him like that, we shall be thieves ourselves."

"Don't be silly," said Traut. "If a chap pinches something from me and I pinch it back, that doesn't make me a thief."

"It does," declared the Professor.

"I never heard such rot," growled Traut.

"I think the Professor's right," said Emil. "If I take something away from someone without his knowing, that would make me a thief. It wouldn't make any difference whose property it was to start with."

"Yes, that's perfectly true," said the Professor. "And now for goodness' sake stop trying to be clever. We've arranged everything we can. We can't know yet just how we shall catch him. We shall have to make plans for that as we go along. But of one thing I am certain – and that is that he must give back the money of his own accord. We'd be fools to try to steal it from him."

"I don't see that," argued little Tuesday. "How can I steal what's my own? What's mine must be still mine, even if it has got into someone else's pocket."

"It's a bit difficult to explain," said the Professor, "and even some grown-ups can't understand it. Morally speaking you may be right, but in the eyes of the law you'd be wrong, and if it came to the point, they'd find you guilty of theft. That's how it is, I'm afraid."

"Oh, have it your own way," said Traut, shrugging his shoulders.

"Do you know how to shadow a man properly?" asked Peters. "If you don't, he'll spot you sure as eggs are eggs – and that would put the lid on everything."

"Yes, you'll need some good sleuths," said little Tuesday. "That's why I thought I'd be so useful. I'm jolly good at shadowing people. I can bark too," he added, with a grin, "so you could have used me as your police dog!"

"I should have thought that would be just the way to draw attention to us in Berlin," Emil said impatiently.

"You ought to have a revolver, you know," Peters went on.

"Oh, yes, we ought to have a gun," echoed one or two others.

"We ought *not*," returned the Professor sharply.

"I bet the thief's got one," said Traut.

"This is a dangerous business all right," said Emil. "Anyone who's afraid had better go home to bed."

"Are you calling me a coward?" Traut asked angrily, putting up his fists.

"Order, order," called the Professor. "Fight tomorrow if you want to, not now. You're behaving like a lot of . . . kids!"

"Well, that's what we are," said Tuesday, and they all laughed.

"I ought to send a few lines to my grand-mother," Emil said rather anxiously. "They'll be wondering where on earth I've got to. They might even go to the police. Could anyone take a note for me while we get on with this business? They live at 15 Schumann Street."

"I'll go," said a boy named Brett. "Write it quickly, so that I get there before they lock up. I'll go by underground if someone will let me have the money."

The Professor gave him fourpence, enough to take him there and back again. Emil borrowed paper and pencil and wrote:

Dear Grandma,

I expect you're wondering what's happened. I arrived in Berlin all right, but I can't come and see you yet because I've something very important to do first. I can't tell you about it now, but don't worry. As soon as everything's settled I'll come straight over. I'm longing to see you. The boy who is bringing this letter is a friend and knows where I am, but he mustn't tell you because it has to be a secret at present.

Love to all,

Your loving grandson EMIL.

P.S. Mummy sent her love, and I've got a bunch

of flowers for you which I'll bring as soon as possible.

He folded the paper over and wrote the address on the other side.

"Don't tell any of them where I am or that I've lost the money," he told Brett. "I'd get into terrible trouble if they knew."

"O.K.," said Brett. "Give it here. When I get back I'll ring Tuesday and find out what's been happening. Then I'll go on and join the reserves." And off he ran.

Meanwhile the five boys had returned with packets of food. Gerold had brought a whole liver sausage, which he said his mother had given him. All five had warned their families that they might be out late. Emil shared out sandwiches, and kept the sausage for another time.

Five more boys then ran home to ask permission to stay out and two of them did not come back. Presumably their parents would not let them.

"We ought to have a password," the Professor remembered suddenly, "so that Tuesday can be sure who we are when we telephone. We can't risk having strangers butting in. Let's make it

'Emil'. That's easy to remember."

Little Tuesday went home then with Traut, the messenger, who was still grumbling. "Best of luck," he said as they went away.

"I say, ring up my father," the Professor called after them. "Tell him I've very important business to attend to. Then he won't worry about me being out late," he added to Emil.

"My word, parents in Berlin are jolly decent," said Emil.

"You needn't think they're all like that," said Krumm, scratching behind his ear.

"On the whole they're pretty reasonable," returned the Professor. "Most of them know that as long as they trust us we aren't likely to deceive them. I promised my father never to do anything mean or dangerous and as long as I abide by that, I can do pretty well as I like. My father's a good sort."

"He must be," said Emil. "But this affair today may be dangerous. Then what?"

"Oh well," said the Professor, with a shrug, "in such cases my father always says 'think what you'd do if I were standing beside you' and I know that's what he'd say today. Now let's be off." He stood up and addressed the rest of the boys.

"Now then, we detectives have to depend on all of you," he said. "Means of communication are established. You all know Tuesday's number. I'm going to leave you my share of the money because we have enough without it. There's one and eightpence left. Just count it, Gerold, will you? We've all got food. Oh – and if anyone wants to go home, he'd better go, but mind there must never be less than five here on duty. See to that too, will you, Gerold? Show what you're made of, boys, and we'll do our best to depend on that. If we need any help, Tuesday will send Traut to tell you. Any questions? No? Everything clear? Don't forget the password, *Emil*."

"Password *Emil*," they shouted, and so loudly, it echoed round the square and made passers-by wonder what was going on.

It was all so thrilling that Emil began to feel almost pleased that his money had been stolen.

# CHAPTER 10

# The Quarry Goes to Ground

Three of the scouts whom Gustav had posted along Trautenau Street now came tearing into Nicholas Square, beckoning frantically to the young detectives.

"Come on," shouted the Professor, and he, Emil, the two Mittlers, and Krumm tore off towards Kaiser Avenue as if they were trying to break the world record for the hundred yards. They slowed down as they approached the newspaper stand and came on more cautiously, as Gustav was making signs of some sort to them.

"Are we too late?" panted Emil.

"Don't be daft," Gustav whispered back. "If I say I'll do a thing, I do it properly."

Then they saw the thief standing on the pavement outside the café, looking about him as though he were in Switzerland, admiring the view. He bought an evening paper from the newsvendor and glanced at the headlines.

"It'll be a bit awkward if he comes this way,"

remarked Krumm. They were hiding behind the news-stand, but keeping a watchful eye on him. They were all agog with excitement. The thief went on reading his paper, and seemed to pay no attention to anything else.

"I believe he's squinting over the top of it to see if he's being watched," said the elder Mittler.

"Did he seem to look your way much while you were waiting?" the Professor asked Gustav.

"No, not once," Gustav replied. "He was too busy eating. You'd have thought he hadn't had a meal for days."

"Look out," cried Emil abruptly.

The man was folding up his paper. He gave a quick glance at the passers-by and hailed a taxi. It drew up, and he got in and slammed the door. By that time the boys had also hailed a taxi, and Gustav said to the driver: "Follow that taxi which is just turning into Prague Place, please, but don't let the man inside it see he's being tailed."

The second taxi moved off, crossed Kaiser Avenue, and kept at a safe distance from the other.

"What's up?" the driver asked.

"He's up to something, and we don't want to lose track of him," explained Gustav. "But that's between ourselves, mind."

"O.K.," said the driver. "How much money have you got?"

"Plenty!" said the Professor with dignity.

"Oh well, I only wondered," said the driver.

"The number of his taxi is IA3733," remarked Emil.

"That's important," said the Professor, making a note of it.

Krumm leaned forward and warned the driver not to get too near.

"Don't worry, I won't," muttered the man.

They drove for some distance along Motz Street, through Victoria Louise Square, and then on down Motz Street again. A few people on the pavement stopped to look at the taxi and laughed at the crowd of boys riding in it.

"Duck down," Gustav ordered suddenly, and they immediately threw themselves higgledy-piggledy on the floor of the taxi.

"What's up?" asked the Professor.

"Traffic lights just going against us," said Gustav, "and his taxi will be held up as well as ours."

The cabs actually stopped one behind the other, to wait for the lights to turn green. The second one appeared to be empty, for the boys were quite hidden. The driver glanced over his shoulder and chuckled at what he saw. When they drove on again the boys cautiously resumed their seats.

"I hope he's not going very far," murmured the Professor, watching the meter anxiously. "It's cost us tenpence already."

But very soon after that, the first taxi stopped in front of the Hotel Kreid in Nollendorf Square. The boys' driver braked suddenly and stopped at a safe distance, so that they could watch what happened next.

The man in the bowler hat got out, paid the driver and disappeared into the hotel.

"Follow him, Gustav," cried the Professor urgently. "If the place has two exits, we'll lose him." Gustav was gone in a flash.

The rest of the boys clambered out, and Emil paid the fare, which was a shilling. The Professor led the way through an archway that stood at the side of a cinema, and went down an alley into a courtyard which ran right along behind the cinema and the Nollendorf Theatre which was next door to it. Then he sent Krumm off to contact Gustav.

"It might be a good thing for us if that chap stays in the hotel," Emil remarked. "This place

The hotel in Nollendorf Square

would make a first-rate head quarters."

"With every modern convenience," agreed the Professor. "There's an underground station just opposite. We've got good cover, and a restaurant over the way with a telephone box. It couldn't be better."

"I hope Gustav will be careful," Emil said.

"You can trust him," said the elder Mittler. "He looks a fool, but he's not."

"I wish he'd hurry, though," said the Professor, sitting down on a chair someone had left in the courtyard, and looking like a general before a battle.

Then Gustav returned, rubbing his hands gleefully. "We've got him!" he said. "He's taken a room at the hotel, and I watched him go up in the lift. There's no other way out. I've checked the whole building, and unless he climbs out over the roof, we've got him trapped."

"Is Krumm keeping watch there?" asked the Professor.

"Yes, of course," said Gustav.

The Professor gave the elder Mittler the money, and sent him to telephone little Tuesday.

"Hullo, Tuesday, is that you?" he said when he got through.

"Speaking," chirped the voice at the other end.

"Password *Emil*. Mittler here. Bowler Hat has taken a room at the Hotel Kreid, Nollendorf Square. We're making our headquarters in the courtyard behind the cinema there."

Little Tuesday wrote it all down, then read it back. "Any reinforcements needed?" he asked.

"No," said Mittler.

"Have you had much trouble so far?"

"Not really, but he took a taxi, and we had to take one too, so as to keep up with him. Now he's gone up to his room at the hotel. He's probably looking to see if there's anyone under the bed, and after that I daresay he'll play cards with himself!"

"What's the room number?" asked Tuesday.

"Don't know yet, but we'll find out."

"Gosh, I wish I was with you. Next time we have to choose a subject to write about at school, I shall use this."

"Has anyone else rung up?"

"Not a soul! It's been frightfully dull."

"Well, goodbye for now."

"Good luck, chaps. Oh lord, I forgot! Password *Emil*."

"Any reinforcements needed?" asked little
Tuesday.

"Password *Emil*," Mittler repeated, and went back to the courtyard to report.

It was now eight o'clock and the Professor went out to inspect the guard.

"We're not likely to get hold of him tonight, dash it!" said Gustav restlessly.

"Well it wouldn't be a bad thing for us if he went straight to bed," Emil pointed out. "If he goes out again and starts taking taxis and going to restaurants or night clubs or a theatre, we shouldn't have enough money to follow him."

The Professor came back and sent the Mittlers out to the square to act as liaison men.

"We've got to think how to keep tabs on that fellow," he said. "Think hard now, will you?"

They all sat still for a time, thinking deeply, until they were interrupted by the sound of a bicycle bell, and a very new and shiny bike came flashing into the courtyard with Pony riding it, and Brett behind her, on the step. They both shouted "Three cheers!" as they saw the others.

Emil jumped to his feet and ran to help them off, recognizing Pony, and they shook hands gaily. "This is my cousin Pony Hütchen – or rather Heimbold," he said.

The Professor politely gave up his chair, and she sat down, but turned on Emil immediately.

"You are a wretch!" she cried. "You come to Berlin – and before you even get off the train, you run smack into the middle of a thriller! We were just going off to the station again, to meet the next train from Neustadt, when your friend Brett turned up with your note. He's all right, by the way. I like him."

Brett blushed and stuck his chest out.

"Mum and Dad and Grandma are all sitting at home wondering what on earth you can be up to. Brett wouldn't tell me anything in front of them of course, so I just said I'd see him downstairs. Then I slipped out of the house with him and came along. But I must dash back at once, or they'll be sending for the police. Their nerves won't stand losing two of us in one day."

Brett held up two pennies. "Pony's bike saved us the return fare," he said proudly, and the Professor put the money back in his pocket.

"Are they furious?" Emil asked Pony.

"Not a bit," she replied. "Grandma got a bit wild, and kept on saying, 'I expect he's just gone to call on the President!' till Mum and Dad seemed to think it was quite possible. I hope you'll catch your man tomorrow though.

Who is your Sherlock Holmes?"

"The Professor," said Emil. "Here he is."

"Nice to meet you," laughed Pony. "I've always wanted to know a real detective."

The Professor laughed too, because he was embarrassed, and mumbled something quite unintelligible.

"Before I go, I'd better give you my pocket money," said Pony. "Here it is – eightpence. Buy yourself a cigar or two with it, boys!"

Emil took the money, but Pony remained on the only chair, like a beauty queen surrounded by the selection committee.

"I really must go," she said at last, "but I'll be back in the morning. Where are you all going to sleep? I wish I could stay! I'd make you some coffee. But I can't, of course. Nice girls like me have to be in bed in good time. Well, goodbye everybody. Goodnight, Emil." She put a friendly hand on her cousin's shoulder, jumped on her bicycle and rode away, ringing her bell like mad.

The boys were quite speechless for a few minutes after she had gone. Then the Professor murmured, "Well, well, well," as his father might have done, and the others thought he was quite right.

# CHAPTER 11

# A Spy in the Hotel

Time seemed to pass very slowly.

Emil went out to see the three guards, hoping they would let him replace one of them, but Krumm and the two Mittlers said they would rather stay where they were. Then he cautiously put his nose round the hotel entrance, in case there was anything to see there, and came back to the courtyard quite excited.

"I tell you what," he said, "we ought to have a spy inside the hotel all night. I know Krumm is watching from the street corner, but he's only got to turn his head away for a moment and Grundeis could slip out and disappear, without our knowing anything about it."

"That's all very well," Gustav replied, "but you can't simply go up to the porter and say you're going to sit on the stairs all night. And if you did get in – supposing old Bowler Hat looked out and recognized you? All our work would be wasted. No, you mustn't show your face inside whatever happens."

"That's not what I meant," said Emil.

"What did you mean then?" asked the Professor.

"Well, there's sure to be an odd-job boy in the hotel – working the lift and all that. I thought one of us might get hold of him and tell him what's going on. He'll know the place like the back of his hand, and could tell us how to keep an eye on that room all night."

"Good," said the Professor. "Very good, in fact." He had a habit of speaking like a schoolmaster, and that had earned him his nickname.

"Good for you, Emil," said Gustav. "Anyone would think you were Berlin born! If you get any more brilliant ideas like that, we'll have to give you the freedom of the city!"

"Berliners aren't the only people with brains," said Emil, not liking to hear Neustadt slighted, and he added, "We still haven't had that boxing match by the way."

"What? What's that?" asked the Professor.

"Gustav insulted my best suit," Emil replied.

"Well, you'd better fight it out tomorrow," the Professor decided. "Tomorrow, or not at all."

"Oh, your suit's all right," Gustav said carelessly. "I've got quite used to it now. I'll fight any time you like, of course, but I warn you, I'm champion in my part of the town, so you'd better look out."

"Well, I'm champion at my school," said Emil.

"Oh, shut up, both of you!" said the Professor. "You and your fists! What I'm concerned about is getting into the hotel, but I suppose I can't leave you two alone, or you'll start hammering each other."

"Let me go then," said Gustav.

"All right," said the Professor. "Go and talk to the lift-boy, but watch your step. See what you can do. You ought at least to find out which room the fellow's in. Come back and report in an hour's time."

Gustav left them, and Emil and the Professor went out and stood in the street by the archway, talking about their schools, and the masters. The Professor pointed out different makes of car as they went by, and told Emil how to recognize them. Then they had a sandwich.

It was getting dark, and the illuminated signs began to flash on and off. Trains thundered by on the overhead railway. Other trains rumbled beneath them on the underground. The noise in the street of all the passing trams, buses, cars and motorbikes sounded to Emil like some crazy orchestra playing wildly. From a nearby café came the strains of dance music, and people were crowding into the cinemas round the square for the last performances.

To Emil it was all strange and tremendously exciting. He almost forgot how he came to be there, and about the seven pounds which had been stolen.

"It's funny to see a big tree like that growing over there by the station," he remarked. "It looks as though it's got there by mistake. Berlin's wonderful, of course, but I don't know that I should like to live here always. Neustadt's small. We have two markets, and the station square, and the playground by the river, and the Amsel Park, and that's all. But it's enough for me. Here it's as noisy as though there was a fair going on all the time – and so many streets and squares – I should always be losing my way. I don't know what would have happened to me tonight, if I hadn't found you chaps. It gives me the creeps just to think of standing here all alone."

"You get used to it," said the Professor, "and I probably shouldn't be able to stick a small place like Neustadt, with its two markets and a playground!"

"You get used to that too," Emil replied.

"Is your mother very strict?" the Professor asked next.

"My mother! Not a bit. She lets me do more or less as I like, but then I mostly don't want to, if you see what I mean."

"I can't say I do," said the Professor.

"Well, it's like this," Emil explained. "Are your people well off?"

"I don't really know. No one ever talks about money at home."

"Then I expect you have plenty," Emil observed wisely.

The Professor thought for a moment, and then said, "I dare say you're right."

"My mother and I talk a lot about money because we've got so little. She has to earn it, and works jolly hard, but even so there's never really enough. Yet when there's anything on, like a school outing, she always manages to give me as much as the other boys have to spend – sometimes more."

"How can she do that?" asked the Professor.

"I don't know, but she does. Of course I always try to bring some back."

"She expects you to, does she?"

"No, nothing of the kind. But I like to."

"I see," said the Professor, "that's the way things work out in your home."

Emil nodded. "Yes, just about. Sometimes I go out in the evenings with Protzsch, who lives on the floor above us, or with some of the other boys, and Mum says I needn't be home till nine. Then I usually get back a bit earlier, perhaps by seven, so that she doesn't have to have supper alone. She says I should stay out with my pals, and I do sometimes. But it isn't much fun when I know she's all by herself, and she's always really pleased to see me back, whatever she may say about it."

"It's not a bit like that in my home," said the Professor. "If by any chance I get home early, I'm sure to find everyone's gone out to dinner or the theatre or something. We're quite fond of each other, of course, but we all go our own ways."

"Well, it doesn't cost anything to be together," Emil said. "But don't you go thinking I'm a mummy's boy or anything like that. I'd bash anyone who said so. See what I mean?"

"Yes, I do," said the Professor.

They stood under the archway in silence for a while. Night came down. The stars were clear and glittering, and the moon seemed to be watching the overhead railway out of one eye.

The Professor cleared his throat, then said, without looking at Emil, "I expect you and your mother are very fond of each other."

"Yes, we are," Emil replied simply.

# Chapter 12

## Two Lift-boys in Green

A detachment of the reserve forces appeared in the courtyard about ten o'clock, bringing with them enough sandwiches to feed a regiment, and asking for further instructions.

The Professor was furious and told them they had no business to come unless they were sent for. "I told you to wait at Nicholas Square," he reminded them, "until Traut brought you word from telephone headquarters."

"Don't be so shirty," said Peters, "we were dying to know how you were getting on."

"Besides, when Traut didn't come we were afraid something must have happened to you," said Gerold by way of excuse.

"How many of the boys are still at Nicholas Square?" Emil asked.

"Three or four," replied Frederick the First.

"About two," said Gerold.

"If you ask them again, they'll say there's no one there at all," cried the Professor angrily.

"Who do you think you are, shouting like that!" exclaimed Peters.

"I propose that Peters is expelled from the corps of detectives and not permitted to take any further part in the case," said the Professor, stamping his foot.

"I'd be sorry if you had a row on my account," said Emil. "Let's take a vote on it, like they do in Parliament. I propose that Peters is let off with a caution. Of course we can't have people running off on their own, whenever they feel like it."

"Stuck-up lot of pigs," said Peters. "I'm going anyway." And he stamped off, muttering something very rude indeed.

"It was his idea," said Gerold. "We'd never have come otherwise. And we left Meyer to hold the fort."

"Let's forget it," said the Professor quietly, returning to his usual manner. "We'll say no more about Peters."

"What shall the rest of us do now?" asked Frederick the First.

"I suggest you wait till Gustav comes back from the hotel with his report," said Emil.

"Good idea," said the Professor. "Look, isn't that the lift-boy coming now?"

"So it is," agreed Emil.

A boy in a green uniform with a cap on the side of his head paused under the archway, and waved to them.

"Smashing uniform," muttered Gerold enviously.

"Have you got a message from our scout, that is, from Gustav?" called the Professor.

The boy nodded and came nearer.

"Well, what is it?" Emil asked impatiently.

Suddenly a motor-horn honked and the boy in green danced about, roaring with laughter.

"You old idiot, Emil!" he shouted. It was Gustav himself, not the real lift-boy.

"You!" exclaimed Emil in amazement, and they all laughed so hard that somewhere up above them a window was opened and a voice yelled to them to be quiet.

"Oh well done, Gustav," said the Professor. "Now quiet, all of you, while you hear all about it."

"It was simply marvellous," said Gustav. "I slipped into the hotel and saw the boy waiting by the lift, so I caught his eye, and over he came to see what I wanted. Then I told him the whole story from A to Z – all about Emil losing his money, and about us, and how the thief was staying in the hotel, and that we have to keep an eye on him so that we can go after him tomorrow and get the money back. He thought it was no end of a lark, and said he'd got a spare uniform I could borrow, and with that I could pretend to be a second lift-boy.

" 'What about the hall-porter?' I asked. 'Won't he mind?'

" 'Not he, he's my father,' he said.

"I don't know what story he told his old man, but I got the uniform all right. What's more, he said I can spend the night in an empty room there, in the servants' quarters, *and* bring one of you with me. How's that? Eh?"

"Did you find out which room the thief is in?" asked the Professor.

"Some people are never satisfied!" exclaimed Gustav. "What do you think I've been doing all this time? It wasn't all that easy, and you haven't heard half of it yet. The boy thought the thief was in Room 61 on the third floor, so I went up and spied out the land a bit. No one saw me. I made sure of that. Then I tucked myself out of sight behind the banisters, and after about half an hour the door of Room 61 opened and out came our thief. I recognized him at once. I'd had a good look at him while I was watching him at the café this afternoon – little black moustache, thin sticking-out ears, and a face ugly as sin.

"He went to the toilet, and as he was coming back I touched my cap and said, 'Will you be wanting anything more, sir?' 'No, nothing,' he said, and then he called me back. 'Wait a minute, though,' he said. 'Yes. Ask the porter to call me in the morning at eight sharp. Room 61. Don't forget.'

"'Very good, sir,' I said, 'I won't forget' – and was I thrilled – 'You'll get a phone call at eight o'clock precisely,' I said. That's the way they call people at this hotel, see? He just nodded and didn't suspect a thing. Then he went on back to his room."

"Excellent," said the Professor, tremendously pleased, and so were the others. "We'll be waiting for him – with a guard of honour – from eight o'clock onwards, and as soon as he appears we'll go after him and have him in the bag in no time."

"He's as good as caught already," laughed Gerold.

"No flowers by request," said Gustav. "Well, I must be off. I've a letter to post for Room 12, and I got sixpence for taking it. Easy money, this job! The regular lift-boy says he sometimes picks up as much as ten bob a day in tips. I'll get up about seven to make sure our thief's called to time. Then I'll report back here."

"I'm so grateful to you, Gustav," Emil said earnestly. "Now everything will be all right, and we can all go to bed. Tomorrow we'll catch the thief and there's nothing to do till then, is there, Professor?"

"No, everyone go home to bed, but be sure you all get back here promptly at eight tomorrow morning. If anyone can get hold of any money, it would be a help. Now I'll ring up little Tuesday, and he can rope in anyone else who reports tomorrow, as extra reserves. We've still got to trap the man, and anything may happen in the process."

"I'd better be the one to sleep in the hotel with you, hadn't I, Gustav?" asked Emil.

"O.K. I expect you'll like that. It's not at all a bad hole."

"I'll go home as soon as I've phoned Tuesday," said the Professor. "I'll send Meyer home too, otherwise he'd sit about in the Square all night waiting for orders. Now, is everything clear?"

"Yes, Chief!" said Gustav with a laugh.

"Report back here promptly at eight a.m.," said Gerold.

"Don't forget about the money, if you can raise any," Frederick the First reminded them.

They all said good night then like business men, solemnly shaking hands all round, and went their various ways. Gustav and Emil went into the hotel. The Professor crossed Nollendorf Square to the telephone box in the restaurant.

One hour later all were asleep, most of them at home in their own beds, but two in a small room on the fourth floor of the Hotel Kreid.

Little Tuesday – tired, but true to his charge – had fallen asleep in his father's armchair beside the telephone. Traut had gone home, but Tuesday would not leave his post and sat on, dreaming of hundreds of telephone calls. At midnight, when his parents came home from the theatre, they were very surprised to find him asleep there. His mother picked him up and carried him to bed. He hardly stirred, but murmured drowsily, "Password *Emil*."

# CHAPTER 13

# Crowd Tactics

The windows of Room 61 of the Hotel Kreid looked out on Nollendorf Square, and while Mr Grundeis was combing his hair next morning he was a little surprised, on glancing down into the square, to see how many children were there. Quite a crowd of boys were playing football on the grass, and more boys were standing in small groups at the corner of Kleist Street and outside the entrance to the underground station. "I suppose it's holiday-time," he thought in disgust, as he put on his tie.

Meanwhile, in the courtyard behind the cinema the Professor had called a meeting, and was letting fly in all directions.

"What's the good of some of us racking our brains to find a way to trap this man," he demanded, "while you lunatics have no more sense than to go and drag in all the kids in Berlin! Can't you see that we simply must not draw attention to ourselves? We're not making a film, and we certainly don't want an audience.

If our man gets away it will be your fault for not keeping your mouths shut."

The other boys stood in a circle round him, listening kindly to the lecture, but not looking in the least conscience-stricken.

"Sorry and all that, Professor," said Gerold. "Don't worry, we'll catch him all right."

"Well, off you go, you silly asses," said the Professor, "and tell those chaps out there to keep out of sight, and away from the front of the hotel. Is that clear? Then quick march."

In a few moments only the detectives were left in the courtyard.

"I borrowed ten bob from the hall-porter," said Emil. "So if the thief tries to break away, we can take a taxi and follow him."

"Why don't you make all those kids out there go home?" asked Krumm.

"You don't suppose they'd go, do you?" the Professor retorted. "They wouldn't budge now if the whole Square blew up."

"There's only one thing for it," said Emil. "We shall have to change our plans. We can't shadow Grundeis as things are. We shall have to hunt him down openly now, using all the extra forces to help us to hem him in. Of course he's bound to see what's happening."

"I'd thought of that, too," said the Professor. "I agree that we must change our tactics, and drive him into a corner so that he has to surrender."

"Oh, jolly good," shouted Gerold.

"He'll probably prefer to hand over the money rather than have a hundred screaming kids running after him wherever he goes, attracting the attention of the whole neighbourhood, and of course of the police too," said Emil.

The others nodded understandingly. Just then the sound of a bicycle bell was heard along the alley, and Pony came pedalling into the courtyard, all smiles.

"Good morning, everybody," she said, as she jumped off her bicycle and unfastened a basket from the handlebars. "I've brought you some breakfast – coffee and rolls – and here's a clean cup too! Oh blow, the handle's come off."

The boys had all had a good breakfast already – Emil had had his in the hotel – but no one wanted to hurt Pony's feelings, so they drank the coffee out of the cup without a handle and ate the rolls as though they had not seen food for a month.

"My word, that was good!" said Krumm.

"Nice crusty rolls," mumbled the Professor with his mouth full.

"Ah," said Pony. "It makes all the difference when there's a woman in the house."

"In the *courtyard*," amended Gerold, who was particular about accuracy.

"How's everything in Schumann Street?" Emil asked.

"All right, thanks. Grandma sends her special love, but she says if you don't come home soon she'll make you eat fish every day you're here as a punishment."

"Ugh, not so good," said Emil, making a face.

"What's the matter with fish?" asked the younger Mittler. The others stared, because little Mittler hardly ever opened his mouth. He blushed a deep red and hid behind his brother.

"Emil can't bear fish. It makes him sick," Pony explained.

They went on talking, feeling very pleased with life, and the boys were all attentive to Pony. The Professor held her bicycle. Krumm took away the Thermos and cup and washed them. The bigger Mittler screwed up the paper bags which had held the rolls, Emil fastened the basket on her handlebars again, and Gerold felt her tyres to make sure they were hard. Meanwhile Pony herself danced about the courtyard, singing and chattering. Then she stopped suddenly, balancing on one leg, and exclaimed:

"Do tell me. What on earth are all those kids doing in the square? It looks like a holiday camp."

"They heard we were out after the thief," the Professor replied, "so they're hanging about to see the fun and join in if possible."

At that moment Gustav dashed into the courtyard, honking his horn furiously.

"Come on," he cried. "He's on his way!"

The others dropped everything, and were rushing off, when the Professor called them back.

"Stop, stop!" he shouted. "Don't forget we have *a plan*! We're going to surround him. Some of you get in front of him, some keep close behind, and the rest crowd in on each side. Got it? There'll be further orders as necessary. Now, forward march!"

They pelted out through the archway into the square, and Pony was left alone in the yard, feeling rather forlorn. Then she jumped on her bicycle and rode after them, muttering, just like her grandmother, "I don't like it! I don't like it at all!"

The man in the bowler hat came out of the

door of the hotel, strolled slowly down the steps to the street, and turned to the right.

The Professor, Emil and Gustav sent messengers back and forth among the children with instructions, and very soon Mr Grundeis found himself completely surrounded.

He looked about in amazement. Boys swarmed round him, all laughing and talking among themselves, jostling each other, yet somehow always keeping up with him. Some of them stared at him so hard that he hardly knew where to look.

Then – whizz – a ball flew past his head. He did not like that, and tried to move more quickly; so did the boys, and he remained surrounded. Then he tried to take them by surprise by turning abruptly to go down a side street, but he could not get through the mass of children which seemed to stream across his path whichever way he turned.

"Just look at his face!" said Gustav. "It's stuck as though he was trying not to sneeze."

"Keep in front of me," said Emil. "I don't want him to recognize me yet. The moment for that will come soon enough."

Gustav threw out his chest and swaggered along like a prize-fighter. Pony pedalled hard, keeping abreast of them and ringing her bell merrily.

The man in the bowler hat was quite clearly getting nervous. He suspected vaguely that he was in danger from this mob of children who had surrounded him. He tried taking tremendously long strides – but that did not help. He stopped in his tracks, turned round and started back the way he had come, but the children did a rightabout turn, too, and he was hemmed in as closely as before.

Then Krumm got right in front of him and tripped him up.

"What do you think you're doing, you clumsy young idiot?" Grundeis shouted. "Get out of my way or I'll call the police."

"Oh, please do," said Krumm politely. "We were hoping you would."

Mr Grundeis, of course, had not the slightest intention of bringing the police into it. At the same time, it was getting past a joke, and he was beginning to feel really alarmed, because he could not see how to get away from all these horrible boys. What was worse, people were beginning to stare out of their windows, and shop assistants were coming out on to the pavement, to see what was going on. If a policeman had come along at that moment, the fat would have been in the fire! The sight of a small branch bank ahead gave him an idea. He broke through the ranks of children successfully, and dashed inside the building. The Professor followed him, but paused at the door to shout back orders.

"Gustav and I'll go in after him. Emil, you stay outside until you hear Gustav's horn. That will mean we're ready. Come inside then, and bring about ten boys with you. Pick them carefully, Emil. It'll be a ticklish job."

Then he and Gustav pushed open the door and walked into the bank.

Emil was so excited he could hardly breathe. This was the moment he had been waiting for. He chose his men – Krumm, Gerold, the two Mittlers, and a few more – and told the rest to scatter. They only withdrew a step or two, however, for they simply could not bear to be out of what was going to happen next.

Pony got one of the boys to hold her bike while she spoke to Emil.

"I'm still here," she said. "Good luck! Things are getting pretty lively now, aren't they? Gosh, I'm so excited, I can't keep still."

"Same here," said Emil.

The sight of a small branch bank ahead gave him an idea.

*The big banks have branches in all parts of the city, where people with money can buy shares, and those with accounts can cash cheques. Sometimes messengers come in for change, and people also go there to exchange their money for that of other countries. Some people even go to the bank at night when there is no one there to attend to them. Then they just help themselves.*

# CHAPTER 14

# Saved by a Pinprick

Inside the bank, Gustav and the Professor saw the man with the bowler hat standing at the counter, in a frantic hurry to be attended to, but the cashier was talking on the telephone.

The Professor edged quietly up beside the thief, watching him like a lynx. Gustav stood just behind him with his hand on the horn in his trouser pocket. When at last the cashier came over to the counter he asked the Professor what he wanted.

"This gentleman was before me," the Professor pointed out politely.

"And what can I do for you?" the cashier asked Mr Grundeis.

"I want some change, please," the thief replied. "Will you give me pound notes for this fiver – oh, and two pounds worth of silver." He handed across the counter first a five-pound note and then two single pounds, all of which he took out of his pocket.

The cashier picked them up and opened his cash drawer.

"Wait a moment!" cried the Professor. "That's stolen money."

"What!" exclaimed the cashier, looking at the boy in astonishment. The clerks at their desks, behind him, stopped adding up their long columns of figures and their heads jerked up as though they'd been bitten by a snake.

"That money doesn't belong to this gentleman," said the Professor. "He stole it from a friend of mine, and he only wants change in order to get rid of the notes in case they are found on him."

"What impudence!" said Mr Grundeis loudly, and added to the cashier, "Excuse me, there's only one answer to that kind of thing."

He raised his hand and gave the Professor a resounding slap in the face.

"That won't help you," said the Professor, and punched Mr Grundeis in the stomach so hard that he had to hold on to the counter.

The bank clerks all got to their feet and came over to see what was happening. Then Gustav honked loudly three times on his horn, and the manager stormed out of his private room just as ten boys, with Emil at their head, burst through the doors and closed in on Mr Grundeis.

"What on earth's going on here?" demanded the manager.

"These young scoundrels have had the impertinence to say I stole some money which I'd just come in here to change," Mr Grundeis explained, literally shaking with anger.

"And so you did," Emil cried, jumping up. "He stole it from me yesterday afternoon – a five-pound note and two pound notes. We were in the train from Neustadt to Berlin, and I had fallen asleep."

"Can you prove it?" asked the cashier sternly.

"I've been in Berlin all the week," put in Bowler Hat, now smiling politely. "I was busy in the City all day yesterday, from morning till night."

"It's not true! It's a lie!" Emil shouted, almost crying with anger.

"Can you *prove* that this gentleman is the one who travelled in the train with you?" asked the manager severely.

"Of course he can't," said the thief scornfully.

"If he was alone in the train with him, of course he wouldn't have any witnesses," remarked one of the clerks, and Emil's friends glanced anxiously at one another.

"I can produce a witness though," Emil suddenly remembered delightedly. "Mrs Jacob from Gross-Grünau. She was in the compartment when I got in, though she got out quite soon afterwards. She asked me to remember her to Mr Kurshals in Neustadt where I live."

"I must ask you to produce an alibi then," the manager said to the thief. "Can you do that?"

"Naturally," said Grundeis stiffly. "I'm staying at the Hotel Kreid across the road."

"But only since yesterday evening," Gustav pointed out. "I know, because I've been there, disguised as a lift-boy, practically ever since he took the room."

At that, a smile seemed to pass over the faces of the bank clerks. They were beginning to be on the side of the boys.

"Well, sir," said the manager, "I'm afraid we shall have to keep the money here for the time being, Mr er ... er ..." and he reached for paper to write down particulars of all that had happened.

"His name is Grundeis," Emil informed the manager.

At that the man in the bowler hat laughed

loudly. "My name is Müller," he said. "They've made a mistake, you see!"

"What lies he tells," Emil exclaimed furiously. "He told me himself in the train that his name was Grundeis."

"Have you any papers to prove who you are?" asked the cashier quietly.

"Not with me, unfortunately," said the thief. "But if you can wait a minute I'll fetch them from the hotel."

"Don't trust him!" screamed Emil. "It is *my* money and I must have it back."

"Yes, yes – but even if what you say is true," said the cashier, "it can't be done as easily as that. How can you prove it really was your money? Did you make a note of the numbers or write your name on the back of the notes?"

"Of course I didn't," Emil replied indignantly. "I never dreamed of it being stolen from me. But it is mine all the same. My mother gave it to me to bring to my grandmother who lives here in Berlin, at 15 Schumann Street."

"Did you happen to notice if any of the notes were marked or damaged in any way?" suggested the cashier helpfully.

Emil shook his head. "No, I didn't," he said.

"Gentlemen," said the thief, "I give you my

word of honour that the money is mine. Do I look the kind of man who would steal from a child?"

Emil suddenly gave a jump.

"Wait a bit," he cried, enormous relief in his voice, "I've thought of something. In the train I pinned the envelope with the money to the inside of my pocket, so there ought to be holes pricked through all the three notes."

There was a gasp, and then silence, while the cashier held the money up to the light. The thief took a sly step backwards. The manager was drumming nervously on the counter with his fingers.

"The boy's right!" said the cashier, quite pale from the strain. "There are − in fact − pinpricks through all these notes!"

"And here's the pin that made them!" added Emil triumphantly, laying the pin on the counter. "I pricked myself with it too."

At this, the thief turned round and, quick as lightning, shoved a way through the boys, so violently that several stumbled and fell over. Then he bolted through the door and was gone.

"After him," cried the manager, and everyone made for the door. But, when they got outside, they saw that the thief had been stopped by more boys. They held on to his arms, and his legs, and his coat. He struggled wildly to free himself, but the boys were too many for him. In the nick of time, a policeman came running towards them. Pony had ridden off on her bicycle to fetch him.

"Arrest that man," said the bank manager. "We have reason to believe that he is a train thief."

The cashier ran back to fetch the money and the pin, and asked for time off. Then he and the policeman, with the thief between them, set off to escort Grundeis to the Police Station, followed by something like a hundred boys.

Pony pedalled along beside them for a time, but when they came to a turning she called out, "Good-bye, Emil old boy, I must be off home to tell them all about it."

"O.K.," said Emil. "Give them my love and say I'll be in for dinner."

As she turned away, she called over her shoulder, "I say, you do look like a school outing!" With which she rode off, ringing her bell madly, as usual.

# CHAPTER 15

# Police Headquarters

That odd procession marched on to the nearest police station, where the policeman who had taken the thief in charge reported the affair to the duty sergeant. Emil filled in many of the details, and had to give his name and address, and the date and place of his birth – and the sergeant wrote it all down in his big ledger.

"And what's *your* name?" he asked the thief.

"Herbert Kiessling," said the man.

At this, Emil, Gustav, and the Professor, who had come in with him, all laughed out loud. The cashier, who had just handed over the seven pounds to the sergeant, joined in.

"He's a fine one," said Gustav. "First he says his name is Grundeis, then Müller, and now Kiessling. I'd like to know what it is really!"

"Silence," growled the sergeant. "We shall soon find out what his real name is."

Then Mr Grundeis-Müller-Kiessling gave his address as the Hotel Kreid and told them when he had been born and where. He said he had no identity papers.

"And where were you before you arrived here yesterday?" asked the sergeant.

"In Gross–Grünau," said the thief.

"I bet that's another lie," said the Professor.

"Silence, you," boomed the sergeant. "Every statement will be checked in due course."

The cashier asked if he could go then, but first he too had to leave his name and address. He patted Emil on the shoulder encouragingly, and went back to work.

"Now, Mr Kiessling," continued the sergeant, "did you steal seven pounds from this schoolboy, Emil Tischbein of Neustadt, yesterday afternoon, while in the train to Berlin?"

"Yes," the thief now admitted glumly. "I don't know what made me do it. He was asleep in the corner and the envelope with the money fell out of his pocket. I picked it up, and meant only to look inside and see what it contained. Then – having no money . . ."

"That's not true, either!" Emil exploded. "I pinned the money into my inside pocket. It couldn't possibly have fallen out."

"And he can't say he had no money," put in the Professor, "or he'd have had to use Emil's to pay for all he ate and drank at that café, and for the taxi he took after that."

"You boys must not interrupt," roared the sergeant. "We'll check everything in good time." And he wrote a lot more down in his book.

"I should be much obliged if you could let me go now, sergeant," said the thief with extreme politeness. "I've admitted my mistake and you know where to find me. But I'm in Berlin on a matter of business, and would like to go and attend to it."

"You've got a nerve!" said the sergeant, and lifting the telephone, he rang the police headquarters and asked them to send a car to collect a train thief who had been caught in that district.

"When will I get my money back?" Emil asked anxiously.

"You'll have to go to police headquarters for that," replied the sergeant. "It'll be settled there."

"I say, Emil," whispered Gustav, "I expect you'll go in a Black Maria!"

"Nothing of the kind!" said the sergeant.

"Have you got any money, young Tischbein?"

"Yes, sir," said Emil. "The boys collected some for me yesterday, and the hall-porter at the Hotel Kreid lent me ten shillings."

121

"Well, upon my word, you know your way about, don't you, you young rascals!" growled the sergeant. But it was a good-tempered growl. "Very well then, Tischbein, take the underground to Alexander Square and report to Sergeant Ludwig there. Then you'll hear what's to happen next, and no doubt get your money back."

"Will it be all right if I go and give the porter back his ten shillings first?" Emil asked.

"Perfectly."

The police car arrived a few minutes later and Mr Grundeis was told to get in. The sergeant gave a copy of his report, with the seven pounds, to the policeman on duty in the car. The pin was attached to the report too. Then the car drove away. Crowds of children were still hanging about on the pavement, and they shouted after the thief, but he took no notice. Indeed, he put his nose in the air, as if he was quite proud of being seen driving in such a car.

Emil shook hands with the sergeant and thanked him for his help. Then he told the boys outside that he would be getting his money back at police headquarters and that the hunt was over. At that, they all went streaming off together, like a flock of sheep. Only the inner corps of detectives went with Emil to the hotel, and on to the underground station to get his train to Alexander Square.

"Don't forget to ring up little Tuesday," he reminded them, "and let him know what has happened." He thanked them then for helping him, and hoped he'd see them again before he went home. "I have to pay back the money you all lent me, too," he ended up.

"Just you try to give the money back – that's all," said Gustav, "and I'll just about – and oh! that reminds me, we still haven't had our fight! You know, about your funny old suit."

"Oh, I'm so happy," said Emil, seizing hold of Gustav with one hand, and the Professor with the other. "Let's call the fight off. I'm so grateful for all you've done, I couldn't bear to hit you!"

"You wouldn't get the chance," Gustav boasted cheerfully.

In the end the three boys went together to police headquarters, and were taken down long corridors and past a great many closed doors to the office of Sergeant Ludwig of the Criminal Investigation Department. He was just eating his mid-morning lunch when they were announced.

"Ahuh," said the sergeant, with his mouth

full. "Emil Stuhlbein, amateur detective. We had a phone call about you. The Superintendent wants a word with you. Come with me."

"My name is Tischbein," Emil corrected him.

"Oh – much the same thing," said the sergeant, taking another bite out of his sandwich.

"We'll wait for you here," the Professor said to Emil.

"Don't be long," added Gustav. "It makes me frightfully hungry to see anyone munching away like that."

Sergeant Ludwig led Emil down more corridors, he turned left, then right, then left again, and finally knocked on a door. A voice called, "Come in," and the sergeant turned the handle, and – still munching – announced, "The young detective, Emil Fischbein. You've had information about him, sir."

"My name is Tischbein," Emil said again.

"Quite a good name too," mumbled the sergeant, giving him such a shove that he almost fell into the room.

The Superintendent was a pleasant man. He made Emil sit down in a comfortable armchair and tell him the whole story very carefully from beginning to end.

"I see," he said gravely, when Emil had

finished. "Well, now you shall have your money back."

"Thank goodness for that," said Emil, heaving a great sigh of relief as he put the notes away in his pocket – and he was very careful indeed this time.

"Now don't you let anyone else steal them!" said the Superintendent.

"I certainly won't," Emil promised. "I'm going to take them straight to my grandmother."

"That's right. I'd almost forgotten about her. I must have your Berlin address. I suppose you'll be staying there a few days longer?"

"Yes, I hope so," said Emil. "The address is 15 Schumann Street, care of Heimbold – that is my uncle's name, and my aunt's too."

"You boys have done a fine job," said the big man, lighting a fat cigar.

"Yes, the other chaps were simply marvellous," said Emil enthusiastically. "Gustav – the one with the motor-horn – and the Professor, and little Tuesday, and Krumm, and the Mittlers and all the rest of them. It was great fun. And the Professor was grand at organizing things."

"Well, you didn't do too badly yourself," said the Superintendent, puffing away at his cigar.

"May I ask you something, please?" Emil

said. "What's going to happen to Grundeis or whatever his name is?"

"He's been taken to the Identification Bureau," was the reply, "to be photographed and have his fingerprints taken. Then we shall see if we've got any record of him already in the Rogues Gallery."

"What's that?" Emil inquired.

"It's where we keep the records of all convicted criminals. We also have fingerprints and footprints and other information of people wanted in connection with various crimes, though still at large. It's quite possible that the man who robbed you has been in trouble before. We may even be looking for him already."

"I see. I hadn't thought of that."

Then the telephone rang. "Excuse me," said the Superintendent very politely, lifting the receiver. "Yes? . . . I've something here that will interest you . . . Come along to my room." And he hung up. "Some gentlemen from the press want to interview you," he said.

"Goodness, what does that mean?"

"They'll ask you a lot of questions."

"Gosh, does that mean my name will be in the papers?"

"I shouldn't wonder. When a schoolboy catches a thief, he becomes news."

There was a knock at the door and four men came in and shook hands with the Superintendent. He told them briefly what had happened to Emil, and they scribbled it all down in their notebooks.

"What a story!" said one of the reporters. "Country Boy turns Detective!"

"I suppose you'll be taking him on as a plain-clothes man!" one of the others suggested, laughing.

"Why didn't you go straight to the police and report your loss?" asked another.

That reminded Emil about Sergeant Jeschke at home, and of his dream, and he began to feel nervous again.

"Well?" asked the Superintendent.

Emil took the plunge. "I chalked a red nose and a moustache on the statue of Grand Duke Charles in Neustadt," he confessed. "So you'd better arrest me, sir."

To his surprise the five men burst out laughing, instead of looking grave as he had expected.

"Bless me!" exclaimed the big man, "we can't go arresting one of our best detectives!"

"What a story! Country Boy turns Detective!"

"Oh, do you mean that? Oh, that is a relief!" Emil sighed heavily, and turned to one of the reporters.

"You don't remember me," he said.

"No, I can't say I do."

"You paid my fare yesterday on a No. 177 tram because I hadn't any money," Emil reminded him.

"Of course, so I did! I remember. And you asked for my address so that you could pay me back the money!"

"Yes, and now I can." Emil put his hand in his pocket, and brought out some pennies. "I'd like to give it to you, please," he said.

"No, no, that's all right," said the young man hastily. "Didn't you tell me your name too?"

"Yes, Emil Tischbein."

"And mine's Kästner," said the journalist, and they shook hands.

"So you're old acquaintances. Splendid!" exclaimed the Superintendent.

"How would you like to come along with me, Emil, and see my newspaper office?" said Mr Kästner. "We could stop at a café on the way and have some cream cakes."

"I'd like to treat you," said Emil.

This amused the journalists very much.

"You are independent," they said.

"No, no, this is on me," said Mr Kästner.

"Thank you very much." Emil was all smiles. "But Gustav and the Professor are waiting for me outside."

"Then they must come too," said Mr Kästner. The other journalists asked a few more questions and noted down Emil's answers. Then one of them asked the Superintendent if he thought the theft was Grundeis's first offence.

"I doubt it," was the reply. "Indeed there may be a big surprise in store for all of us there, and if you ring me up in an hour's time, gentlemen, I may have news for you."

Then they all said good-bye, and Emil went back with Mr Kästner to Sergeant Ludwig's room. He was still eating, but greeted Emil cheerfully. "Oh ho, back again, young Uberbein," he said.

"*Tischbein*," said Emil.

They picked up Gustav and the Professor, and Mr Kästner bundled the boys into his car and drove them to a café. On the way Gustav honked his horn and the others were delighted when it made Mr Kästner jump. The café was first-rate. They had cherry slices with masses of whipped cream, and told Mr Kästner all about their adventures – about the council of war in Nicholas Square, and having to follow the thief in a taxi, and the night in the hotel when Gustav was disguised as a lift-boy, and of the terrific row at the bank.

"Well, you really are grand chaps," said Mr Kästner at the end of the story, and they felt so pleased with themselves that they had another round of cherry slices.

Then they separated, and Gustav and the Professor went home by bus, promising to ring up little Tuesday, and Emil drove with Mr Kästner to his office.

The building in which the newspaper was printed was a huge place, almost as big as the police headquarters, and far busier. People kept scuttling to and fro in the corridors as though they were running in an obstacle race. They went into a room where a pretty fair-haired girl was sitting at a desk. Mr Kästner immediately began to dictate Emil's story to her, and she took it straight down on the typewriter. He walked about the room as he dictated, and every little while he asked Emil, "Is that right?" and Emil nodded, and then the typing went on again.

At the end of it he rang up the Superinten-dent, and Emil heard him say:

A huge place, almost as big as the police headquarters.

*Anything a little out of the ordinary may get printed in the newspaper. No one wants to hear about all the calves born with four legs, but if one comes into the world with five or six – and it has been known – why then people want the news to be in their morning papers. Again, if Mr Miller is an ordinary, decent chap, nobody wants to hear about him. But if he waters the milk, and offers the queer stuff as "cream", it's sure to get into the papers, and nothing he can do will prevent it. If you ever go by a newspaper office at night, you'll hear such a clattering and clanging that the very walls will seem to be shaking.*

"What's that? . . . Well, isn't that amazing? . . . Not? All right I won't say a word . . . What? . . . As well? . . . Delighted to hear it . . . Thanks very much . . . That's a story all right!" He hung up and looked at Emil almost as if he had never seen him before.

"We must have a picture of you, Emil. Come along, quick."

"Gosh!" exclaimed Emil, greatly surprised. "A picture? Me? Why?" But he went obediently with Mr Kästner up three floors in the lift, and then into a very brightly lit room with several large windows. Emil tidied his hair and then his photograph was taken.

Finally they went to the compositors' room, where there was a clatter like a thousand type-writers at work all at once. Mr Kästner gave a man there the pages which the fair-haired girl had typed.

"This is a very important story," he said. "I'll be back in a minute to discuss it. I've just got to send this nipper back to his grandmother."

Then they went down in the lift to the ground floor and out into the street. Mr Kästner hailed a taxi and put Emil inside.

"Take this young man to 15 Schumann Street as quick as you can," he said, and gave the driver his fare – which Emil did not like. Then he and Emil shook hands. "Give your mother my kind regards when you get home again," he said. "She must be a pet."

"Yes, she is," Emil replied.

"Oh, and another thing," Mr Kästner called as the taxi started off. "Be sure you get hold of this evening's paper and read what it says. You'll have the surprise of your life."

Emil leaned out of the window to wave to him, and Mr Kästner waved back until the taxi swung round a corner and was out of sight.

# CHAPTER 16

# Emil Has Money to Spend

As the taxi was going down the famous Berlin street called Unter den Linden, Emil knocked three times on the glass partition which separated him from the driver, and the car stopped immediately.

"Are we nearly there?" he asked.

"Yes," said the driver.

"I'm awfully sorry to trouble you but I've just remembered my suitcase and the bunch of flowers for my grandmother. I left them at the Café Josty in Kaiser Avenue yesterday, and I'll have to fetch them. Will you please take me there first?"

"Well, that depends," said the taxi-man. "How much money have you got, in case what the gentleman gave me isn't enough?"

"Oh, plenty," said Emil cheerfully, "and I must have those flowers."

"All right," said the driver, and he turned the taxi round and drove through the Brandenburg Gate and the city park to Nollendorf Square.

Now that everything was all right, the Square seemed to Emil quite a harmless and pleasant place, but all the same he put his hand in his breast pocket to make sure his money was still there. They drove along Motz Street, then turned right and stopped outside the café. Emil went in and asked the girl behind the counter to give him the flowers and the suitcase which had been left there the day before. She handed them over and he thanked her, and got back into the taxi.

"That's all right," he said. "Now we can go on to my Grandma's."

The taxi turned round and drove back the way they had come. They crossed the river Spree, and went through some very old streets, and past some old grey houses, and Emil wished he could have got a better look at them — but he was having trouble with the suitcase, which would keep toppling over. And the draught from the open window tugged at the paper round the flowers till he was half afraid that flowers and all would be blown right out of the taxi.

Then the driver braked suddenly and stopped outside 15 Schumann Street.

"Well, here we are," said Emil, and got out. "What about the fare?"

"As it happens, I've got sixpence change for you," said the driver.

"Keep it," said Emil grandly. "Buy yourself a cigar."

"Thank you, my boy," said the man, "but I don't smoke, I chew." And he drove away.

Emil's relations lived high up in a block of flats and he had to walk up three flights of stairs. As soon as he rang the bell, there were sounds of excitement within. Then the door flew open, and there stood Grandma. She seized him by the shoulders, gave him a kiss on one cheek and a friendly slap on the other, and pulled him inside exclaiming, "Well, you young scamp, you!"

Then Aunt Martha appeared, saying, "Well, well! Nice stories we've been hearing about you, my boy!"

Pony came out of the kitchen, wearing one of her mother's aprons, and held out an elbow for him to shake. "Look out, my hands are wet," she said by way of greeting. "I'm just doing the washing up. Woman's work is never done."

Then they all went into the sitting-room and Emil had to sit on the sofa while his grandmother and his aunt looked at him as though he were an oil painting in a picture gallery.

Emil's grandmother looked at him.

*She is the jolliest grandmother I know, though her life has been a hard one. Some people find it easy to be cheery, and others don't. Emil's grandmother used to live with his parents before his father died. After that Mrs Tischbein found she could not earn enough to keep three people, and the old lady went to Berlin to live with her other daughter. She writes often to Emil and his mother, and ends all her letters, "I am quite well, and hope this finds you the same."*

"Have you got the money?" Pony inquired eagerly.

"Of course," and Emil brought it out of his pocket, and gave the five-pound note and one of the pound notes to his grandmother. "Here it is, Grandma, with Mum's love. She says you mustn't be cross that she hasn't sent you any these last few months, but business wasn't very good. She's sent a little more than usual to make up."

"Thank you, my dear boy," said the old lady, and she gave him back the pound note. "That's for you, for being such a good detective."

"Oh no." Emil drew back. "I can't take it. I really can't. I've still got a whole pound that Mum gave me for myself."

"You just do what your grandmother tells you," she replied. "Put the money in your pocket, and say no more about it."

"I can't do that," Emil protested.

"Don't be silly," said Pony. "*I* shouldn't have to be asked twice!"

"No, really, I'd rather not," he insisted.

"Here, take it, or you'll make me angry," the old lady said, "and that'll bring on my rheumatics."

"Take it and be done with it!" said Aunt

Martha, pushing the pound note into his pocket.

"Well, all right," Emil yielded doubtfully, "if that's how you feel about it – thank you very much, Grandma."

"I have much to be thankful for," she returned, stroking his hair.

Then Emil gave her the flowers, and Pony fetched a vase for them – but when they were unwrapped, nobody knew whether to laugh or cry.

"Oh dear, they look like a bunch of dried herbs," wailed Pony.

"They've had no water since dinner time yesterday," said Emil sadly, "so it's not surprising that they're dead. But they were quite fresh when Mum and I bought them."

"I'm sure they were," said Grandma and she put them in the vase.

"They may revive," Aunt Martha said consolingly. "Now let's have dinner. Uncle won't be home till the evening. Lay the table please, Pony."

"All right. Guess what we're having, Emil."

"I've no idea," he replied.

"What do you like best?"

"Macaroni cheese with ham."

"Well, that's exactly what we're having!"

That was what Emil had had for dinner only the day before, but after all that had happened, it seemed more like a week since he had sat down to it with his mother in Neustadt. As a matter of fact, he would not have minded sitting down to it every day of the week, so now he tucked into it as heartily as if he had been Mr Grundeis-Müller-Kiessling!

After dinner Emil and Pony went out into the street for a time, as Emil wanted to try her grand new bicycle. Grandma lay down to rest on the sofa, and Aunt Martha went into the kitchen to bake one of her famous apple cakes.

Emil rode up and down Schumann Street, with Pony running behind, holding on to the saddle because she said she was afraid he might fall off. Then he watched while she got on and circled round in figures of eight and three.

Presently a policeman came towards them, and said, "Do either of you know which is the Heimbolds' flat? Is it No. 15?"

"That's right," said Pony. "And I'm Pony Heimbold. Wait a moment and I'll show you." And she hastily wheeled her bike away to the basement.

"Is anything the matter?" Emil asked. The

thought of Sergeant Jeschke still preyed on him.

"Oh no, quite the contrary," said the policeman. "You wouldn't by any chance be Emil Tischbein, would you?"

Emil nodded.

"Well, you are certainly to be congratulated."

"What's that? Is it anyone's birthday?" asked Pony, coming back in time to hear the last words.

But the policeman would not tell them anything more, and they climbed the stairs in silence. Aunt Martha opened the door and took them into the sitting-room. Grandma was awake now, and sat up at once, full of curiosity. Emil and Pony stood by the table, eager and expectant.

"It's like this," said the policeman. "The thief who was tracked down this morning, thanks to Emil Tischbein, has been identified as the man who robbed a big bank in Hanover last month. We've been searching for him for some time. Now he has made a full statement, and most of the money has been found sewn into the lining of his jacket – all in one-hundred-pound notes."

"Whew!" exclaimed Pony.

"A fortnight ago the bank offered a reward

for the capture of the thief," the policeman went on. "You caught him," he said to Emil with a meaning nod, "so the reward is yours. And the Superintendent asked me to give you his kind regards, and to tell you he is very glad to see courage and enterprise rewarded in this way."

Emil made a little bow. He could not think of anything else to do.

The policeman then took a wad of bank notes out of his pocket book and counted them out on to the table. Aunt Martha's eyes followed every movement, and her lips shaped the numbers as she counted with him.

"Fifty pounds," she murmured, as he slapped the last note down.

"My goodness!" exclaimed Pony.

It was Grandma who signed the policeman's receipt, and before he went away Aunt Martha gave him a glass of cherry brandy which she brought out of Uncle's cupboard.

Emil sat down on the sofa by his grandmother, quite speechless, and she put her arm round him.

"I can hardly believe it," she said, shaking her head, "I can hardly believe it."

Pony got up on a chair and pretended to be conducting a band. "Now we'll invite, now we'll invite, all the other boys to tea," she sang.

"Yes, we can do that," Emil said, finding his voice at last. "But first of all ... Oh, what fun! ... I can, can't I? Let's make Mum come to Berlin too!"

# CHAPTER 17

# Mrs Tischbein Is Sent For

Mrs Wirth, the Neustadt baker's wife, went along to Mrs Tischbein's early next morning, and rang her doorbell.

"Good morning," she said when the door opened. "How are you, Mrs Tischbein?"

"Oh good morning, Mrs Wirth," Emil's mother replied. "I'm so worried. I haven't heard a word from my boy since he went away. Each time the bell rings I feel sure it must be the postman, but no! Do you want to make an appointment?"

"No, no," said the baker's wife. "I've just come to bring you a message."

"Oh yes? That's very kind of you."

"It's from Emil. He sends his love and . . ."

"Merciful heavens! Has anything happened to him? Where is he? How did you hear? What is it all about?" Mrs Tischbein was so frantic, she could hardly wait for the rest of the message.

"Now it's all right, my dear," said Mrs Wirth soothingly. "Emil's perfectly all right. But would you believe it! He went and caught a bank thief! And there was a reward out for him, and Emil's got it – fifty pounds! What do you say to that, eh? And they want you to go to Berlin on the midday train."

"How do you know . . ." Mrs Tischbein asked weakly.

"Your sister, Mrs Heimbold, rang us up at the shop, and asked me to take you the message. Emil spoke to me himself, too. And they want you to go at once – today. You'll be able to, won't you? – now that Emil has all that money."

"Oh yes, I suppose so," replied Mrs Tischbein vaguely, hardly knowing whether she was on her head or her heels. "Fifty pounds? For catching a thief? What on earth made him do a thing like that? He does do such stupid things."

"Not so stupid this time surely. Fifty pounds is a lot of money," Mrs Wirth pointed out.

"Don't keep on so about the money," said Mrs Tischbein fretfully.

"Well, worse things can happen on a holiday! Are you going to Berlin?"

"Yes, of course I am. I shan't have a moment's peace until I have my eye on him again."

"I hope you'll have a pleasant journey. And enjoy yourself!"

"Thank you, thank you, Mrs Wirth," said Mrs Tischbein, shutting the door and shaking her head slowly from side to side in her astonishment.

Sitting in the train to Berlin that same afternoon, she had an even greater shock. She was very nervous and restless, and kept looking round the compartment, and out of the windows, trying to count the telegraph poles as they flashed by. The train seemed to go so slowly, she wanted to get out and push it. Opposite her sat a man reading a newspaper, and presently her roving eye caught sight of something in it which produced a loud "Merciful goodness!" and she snatched the paper out of his hand. He thought she must have gone mad.

"There!" she cried. "Look! Emil! my son!" and she pointed to a photograph on the front page.

"Really, is that so?" said the man, relieved and interested. "Fancy you being that boy Tischbein's mother! Allow me to congratulate you, Mrs Tischbein!"

"Not at all, not at all," she replied mildly, for she was already beginning to read what the paper said. First, in large letters, were the words:

## FEAT OF BOY DETECTIVE

### 100 BERLIN CHILDREN CHASE THIEF

Then followed a detailed account of Emil's exciting adventures, from the time he left Neustadt until he reached Police Headquarters in Berlin. Mrs Tischbein grew quite pale as she read it. The paper shook in her hands as though she were sitting in a high wind, but in fact both the windows were tight shut. The man could hardly wait for her to finish, but Emil's story filled almost the whole of the front page – including his picture stuck right in the middle of the print – and it took his mother a long time to read it through.

At last she put the paper down and said, "The moment he gets off on his own, he goes and does a thing like that!" She sounded quite exasperated. "And I'd warned him particularly to take care of the money! I don't know how he could have let it happen. He knows how little we have – and he lets the whole lot –

seven pounds – be taken out of his pocket by a thief!"

"Why, he was tired and fell asleep," said the man. "The thief may even have hypnotized him. It's been done before now, you know. But don't you think it was remarkable the way those boys managed everything? A touch of genius there, in my opinion. It was magnificent – simply magnificent."

"Well, I suppose it was," Mrs Tischbein admitted, feeling pleasantly flattered. "Emil's a clever boy, and works hard. He's always top of his class. But supposing something had gone wrong! It makes my hair stand on end to think of it, though I know it's all over now, and everything has really turned out all right. I'll never let him go away alone again, that's certain. I'd die of fright, wondering what was happening to him."

"Is the photograph like him?" asked the man.

"Yes, it's very like him. Do you think he's nice-looking?"

"I do, indeed," said the man. "He looks a fine boy, and I'm sure he'll grow up into a fine man."

"He might have taken more care about his picture," his mother grumbled. "His jacket's all creased. I'm always telling him to unbutton it before he sits down, but he doesn't take a bit of notice."

"Well, if that's his worst fault ..." the man said with a laugh.

"Oh, he's a good boy. He hasn't any really bad faults," said his mother, and was so overcome that she had to blow her nose.

The man got out at the next stop, but he left her the paper, so she read the story of Emil's adventures over and over again until the train reached Friedrich Street station. She read it eleven times altogether.

Emil was waiting for her when she arrived, and he had put on his good suit in her honour. "What do you think of it all?" he asked as he gave her a hug.

"Now don't you start getting conceited about it," she warned him.

"Oh, dear Mrs Tischbein," he said, "I'm so glad you've come," and he put his arm through hers.

"Your thief-hunting hasn't improved the look of your suit," she remarked, but she did not sound in the least cross.

"I could get a new one now – if it was all right by you."

"And where from, may I ask?"

"Some shop wants to give suits to me and Gustav and the Professor," Emil told her, "because then they could say in the papers that we detectives get all our suits from them. For the advertisement, see?"

"I see," said his mother.

"But I expect we'll refuse them," he said grandly, "– though they did say we could have a football each instead of a rotten old suit. But we think all this fuss they're making is jolly silly. Grown-ups seem to like that sort of thing – but we've got more sense."

"Bravo!" said his mother.

"Uncle locked up the money. Fifty pounds! Isn't that wonderful? The first thing we'll do is to get you an electric hair-dryer and a proper winter coat with fur on it. I haven't decided what to get for myself yet. Perhaps a football. Or a camera. We'll see."

"I'm not sure that we ought not to put the money in the bank," said his mother thoughtfully. "You may be glad of it later on."

"You're going to have that dryer and the coat anyway," Emil insisted stoutly. "We can save what's left over if you like."

"We'll discuss it later," said his mother, squeezing his arm.

"Did you know they had my picture in all the papers," Emil asked, "and printed lots of stuff about us too?"

"I read one of them in the train," said his mother. "I was dreadfully upset at first. You're quite sure you're all right, Emil?"

"Of course. It was marvellous! I'll tell you all about it later. But you must see the other boys first."

"Where are they?"

"At Aunt Martha's. She made a huge apple cake yesterday, and invited all the chaps to come round this afternoon. They're there now, making no end of a row, I bet."

It certainly was a noisy party at the Heimbolds', with Gustav, the Professor, Krumm, the Mittlers, Gerold, Frederick the First, Traut, little Tuesday and several more. There were hardly enough chairs for them all. Pony Hütchen was running from one to another with a huge pot of hot chocolate, and Aunt Martha's apple cake was a dream! Grandma was sitting on the sofa laughing at them all, and looking ten years younger.

When Emil came in with his mother, they were given a rousing welcome. Emil introduced the boys, and Mrs Tischbein shook hands with

It was certainly a noisy party, and Aunt Martha's
apple cake was a dream!

each of them and thanked them for being so kind to him.

"I say," he said, "I vote we don't take those suits or the footballs. They're only doing it for advertisement, aren't they?"

"Yes, that's what we think," agreed Gustav, honking his horn so loudly that Aunt Martha's flower pots rattled!

Then Grandma rapped with her spoon on her gold-rimmed tea cup and said:

"Listen to me, boys. There's something I want to say. No. I'm not going to tell you how clever you are. You've had enough of that from other people to turn your heads completely. I'm not going to do that. No, I'm not going to do that."

Everyone kept quite still. They did not even go on eating.

"It does not strike me as so terribly clever to catch a man, when you had about a hundred other children to help you. I hope that does not hurt your feelings." She smiled round on them all pleasantly. "There was one of you, however, who would have simply loved to go trailing after Mr Grundeis, and to have got himself up in a lift-boy's uniform. But he promised to stay at home, and did so because he had promised."

Everyone looked at little Tuesday, who had gone a deep red with embarrassment.

"Yes, little Tuesday." Grandmother nodded towards him. "He sat indoors by the telephone for two whole days because it was his duty. And there wasn't much fun in that, but I call it really fine. And I hope the rest of you will profit by his example. I'd like to see you all stand up and give three cheers for little Tuesday."

The boys jumped up with a will, and Pony cupped her hands round her mouth to make more noise. Aunt Martha and Emil's mother came in from the kitchen, and they all shouted together, "Three cheers for little Tuesday. Hip, hip, hooray!"

Then they all sat down. Little Tuesday took a deep breath and said, "Thanks awfully. But it was nothing really. Don't say any more about it, please."

"Who wants more chocolate?" cried Pony, holding up the big jug. "We must all drink to Emil now."

# CHAPTER 18

# And the Moral of That Is . . .

It was late in the afternoon before the party was over. Before the boys left Emil promised to take Pony to tea with the Professor the next afternoon. Soon afterwards Mr Heimbold came home and they had supper. When it was over he fetched the fifty pounds out of his cashbox and gave it to Mrs Tischbein.

"If I were you I should put it safely in the bank," he told her.

"That's just what I mean to do," she replied.

"Oh no," cried Emil. "That wouldn't be any fun for me! I want Mum to get herself an electric dryer and a coat with a fur collar. It's my money. It was given to me. Can't I do what I like with it?"

"You certainly cannot," declared his uncle. "You're only a child, and you can't touch it. Your mother must decide what's to be done with the money."

Emil got up and went across to the window.

"You are silly, Dad," said Pony. "Can't you see

that Emil wants to give his mother a present? Grown-ups are frightfully dense sometimes."

"Of course she must have the dryer and the coat," put in Grandma. "But you'll let the rest of the money go into the bank, won't you, my boy?"

"Oh yes," said Emil, turning back to them. "That's perfectly all right, if Mum says so."

"All right, you young millionaire! I give in."

"We'll go shopping first thing in the morning," said Emil contentedly. "You'll come too, Pony, won't you?"

"Of course I will," said his cousin. "As if I'd stay at home fly-catching, while you go out shopping! But you must get something for yourself too, after you've got the hair dryer for Auntie. Why not a bike, then mine won't get smashed up with you riding on it!"

"Emil, you haven't broken Pony's bicycle, have you?" asked his mother anxiously.

"Of course not, Mum. I only raised the saddle a bit. It was too low for me, and I had to crouch over the handlebars like a racing cyclist."

"Well, I declare!" exclaimed Pony. "If you mess about with my bike again, I'll never have anything more to do with you."

"If you weren't a girl, and skinny at that, I'd

157

teach you a few things, Pony Hütchen. But I won't quarrel with you today. And anyway it's no business of yours what I buy or don't buy with my own money," and Emil stuck his hands in his trouser pockets with a truculent air.

"That's enough, you two," Grandma put in. "This is no time for squabbling." And the matter was dropped.

Later on Mr Heimbold "took the dog out for a run". They had no dog as a matter of fact, but when her father went out for a glass of beer in the evening, Pony always said he was taking the dog out. Grandma, with Emil and Pony and their mothers, went over all the exciting events of the last two days once more.

"Well, no pain without some gain, they say," Aunt Martha said at last.

"I've learnt something anyway," said Emil. "I shan't be likely to trust a stranger again."

"It's shown me," said his mother, "that children shouldn't be allowed to travel alone."

"Nonsense," said Grandma gruffly. "You're quite wrong there, quite wrong."

"Nonsense, nonsense, nonsense!" cried Pony riding round the room astride a chair.

"So you don't think there's anything to be

learnt from all that's happened?" said Aunt Martha.

"Oh I hope so, I hope so," said Grandma.

"What then?" the others asked with one voice.

"Money should always be sent through the post!" said Grandma, with a merry, tinkling little laugh.

"Three cheers!" cried Pony, and steered her chair out through the sitting-room door.

# CLASSICS TO TREASURE

## From Random House Children's Books

*Also available to collect:*

The Story of **Doctor Dolittle**

HUGH LOFTING

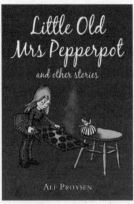

**Little Old Mrs Pepperpot** and other stories

ALF PRØYSEN

**Emil** and the **Detectives**

ERICH KÄSTNER

The **Silver Sword**

IAN SERRAILLIER

The Wolves of Willoughby Chase

JOAN AIKEN

The incredible adventures of **Professor Branestawm**

NORMAN HUNTER

# CLASSICS TO TREASURE
### From Random House Children's Books

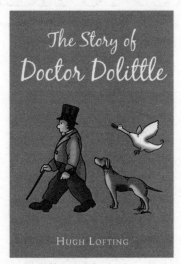

*Once upon a time, many years ago – when our grandfathers were little children – there was a doctor, and his name was Dolittle – John Dolittle M.D.*

Doctor Dolittle likes animals. In fact, he likes them so much he fills his house with every kind of creature imaginable and even learns to talk their language. And when the Doctor hears of a terrible sickness among the monkeys in Africa, soon he and his animal friends are setting off on the most unforgettable adventure . . .

These classic stories of the most extraordinary animal doctor there ever was continue to delight and captivate generation after generation.

# CLASSICS TO TREASURE

**From Random House Children's Books**

Welcome to the wonderfully nutty, fabulously entertaining mishaps of Professor Branestawm!

Professor Branestawm is madly sane and cleverly dotty. He simply hasn't got the time to think about ordinary things – his head is too full of brilliant ideas and wild inventions. Yet the professor's absent-mindedness means that his devices rarely seem to work as they should, and wacky mishaps are never far behind . . .

These ingenious stories have delighted generations of children, and are as timelessly hilarious today as they ever were.

# CLASSICS TO TREASURE

**From Random House Children's Books**

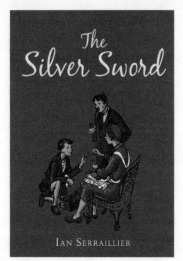

The night the Nazis come to take their mother away, three children escape in a terrifying scramble across the rooftops. Alone in the chaos of Warsaw they have to learn to survive on their own.

Then they meet Jan, a ragged boy with a paperknife – the silver sword – that they recognize as belonging to their lost father. The sword becomes their symbol of hope as, with Jan, they begin the hazardous journey across war-torn Europe to find their parents.

Ian Serraillier's moving account of a family torn apart by war speaks as much to us today as it did when it was first written.

# CLASSICS TO TREASURE
## From Random House Children's Books

Even the wolves that surround the great house of Willoughby Chase are not as cruel and merciless as the evil Miss Slighcarp. So when Bonnie and Sylvia Green, newly orphaned, are left in her neglectful care, they must use all their wits to survive.

The first title in the now classic Willoughby Chase saga is set in 1832 in a period of English history that never happened. King James III is on the throne and a newly opened Channel Tunnel gives access to packs of ravaging wolves…